Stained Glass

*Thought-Provoking Short
Stories and Poems*

by

Janet Hanna

WESTBOW
PRESS
A DIVISION OF THOMAS NELSON

WestBow Press books may be ordered through booksellers or by contacting:

WestBow Press
A Division of Thomas Nelson
1663 Liberty Drive
Bloomington, IN 47403
www.westbowpress.com
1-(866) 928-1240

ISBN: 978-1-4497-8391-4 (sc)
ISBN: 978-1-4497-8390-7 (e)

Library of Congress Control Number: 2013902070

Printed in the United States of America

WestBow Press rev. date: 3/1/2013

Contents

A Different Economy

As the mother listened to the prognosis of her hew born,
the big doctor words just sounded big after a while.
She knew the painful facts.
Her baby would need help for the rest of her life.
She would be scorned and shunned and rejected by other children.
From the hospital chair she looked deep into her own heart. Was
there sin in her life that had caused this? Some lingering thing from
her past still walking around in her body that made the handicap so
pronounced?
Years passed along with several relationships and she finally adjusted
herself to pushing her daughter in a wheel chair.
They were in the mall when someone stopped her and said..
"Do you think your lack of faith caused this?"
"You know" she continued "If you had deeper conviction your
daughter could be healed and walk".
And you know?
At precisely that moment God spoke.
"Man looks at the outer appearance, but I look at the heart."
"My ways are not your ways and My thoughts are not your thoughts".

When the mother opened her mouth she calmly said.
"It's a different economy is all."
In this realm of what we see and touch and taste, hear and smell..we
build it all on a very different economy.
We consider ourselves the healthy normal ones so independent, so
capable of feeding ourselves, moving by ourselves.
And I have often thought...
All God has wanted to do was be the one who feeds us
He wants to be the one who cleans us after we mess ourselves up
He wants to be the one, the only one who provides dignity of life
security and safety....
and you know?
All God has ever wanted to do was push us around in a chairs.

Christ Wore Glasses

I just wonder how to thank the mother who gave you birth?

How do I go to that elementary school and pull up a tray with the
carton of 2% milk
chicken nuggets and a carrot stick and say,
"Excuse me, but one day you'll give birth to a gifted doctor."
Now how do I do that?
Huh?
Which one of those young men throwing spit balls
And spoonfuls of potatoes really understands that in time they will
diagnose our world?
How do we choose?
Should I say, "Only you?"
but not this one.
Would I have known you in a crowd?
Little kid with glasses, nose stuck in a book?
Would your face have made me stop to prematurely say
"Thank You ....Thank you in advance for you will be great someday?"
"It will be your prayers, your devotion to Science, your struggles with
failure that will end up...
saving me.

Now, how does someone pick the school, the neighborhood, age and
child?
I would have known you though...it would have been your eyes to give
you away.
For long ago before either of us were born the sacredness of life and its
power to create life
along with the power to continue creating life came to be.

His eyes became yours and that's funny you know?
Because I didn't know Christ wore glasses.

I Was the Moth

I was at a quaint little cafe last weekend. The place was set deep in the woods. A man ran a shuttle rope out to the main road. There people would park their cars, gather a package of their belongings, choose a knot on the shuttle rope and be led down the trail to the cafe. He, the owner held onto the lead knot with his right hand and an oil lantern in his left hand. The man told stories along the way. Stories of the old country when he was a fisherman. How the nets would fill so full they would break. It took all twelve of them to hoist the nets over the sides of the boats. He told of high fives and smiles and joy at catching that many fish. He spoke of his mother and father who went to a census counting in the middle of her pregnancy. How they travelled such distances to be able to be citizens. He spoke of their youth and the dangers they faced. He would often set the lantern down to wipe tears away. We were hungry. The thing was, we didn't know if it was for another story or food. Then I noticed the lantern covered with luna moths. The light danced and eerily filtered through the green wings. I knew what the moths saw....they saw light and warmth and a guide so sure and strong leading them to a place of refreshment and song. I saw the guide as a type of Christ. And I? I was the moth.

A Natural

The man was a natural
Born to hit that little white ball over hills
Around sand
And stretching it wide
Past lakes of water
And fish....
Made it look so easy...
He was a natural.

She, deaf at birth
Heard music anyway
And when she danced
Or twirled
And sent those silken skirts
Floating through the air...
It took our breath away
She listened to the rhythm in the
Wood
And made it all look so beautifully easy
She too
A natural.
He figured it all in his
Head.
Math problems ten miles long
With fifteen x quotients
And fifty more y axis thrown in
And the chalk would fly and dust would fall
And in moments the problem
Solved
A Natural
That was what he was.

I wonder why some of us
Just are not born with something
Natural
We are conceived the same
Birthed the same

Have two arms..
Two feet
And two of everything else ...
Including left thumbs

I have to believe that that was the whole reason God sent his Son
Christ
He just knew...
We were natural
And
He was
Right.
Natural at
Finding faults
Jostling justifications
Cooly condemning
Berating brothers
Breaking rules
And
Pridefully parading
Around in the
Natural.
So he
Sent the only answer...
His supernatural Son.
Someone who went the distance
Danced to the music of angels
Knew the "y" behind the "x" and
All the dust that settles because of His knowing.
He writes the book...
And signs it with His blood.
So, when you are faced with natural, raw talent....
And you get to thinkin' you're
Really something?
Remember there's a whole bunch
Of natural, raw sin that goes along with it.

A Picture of Us All

As I look around the room
Friendly faces see
There are shades of colors in your eyes
None of them like me

And as I stare at each of them
Some blue and others brown
I notice there are different faces too
Some with smiles and some with frowns.

On our backs some are thrift and others not
But no matter what we wear
Clothes cant cover the character we have not got

For you see now you surely do
The ways we judge and spread the news
The gossip the words
And actions that we choose....

You shake your head
And sweep this with a broom
But do not judge each other
As you look around the room.

For just as you and I are sitting here
Like proud peahens of the south
There are kids in our rooms like each of us
So be extra careful to watch your mouth.

For she may be from a painful home
Where screaming is the norm
And to hear you do the same?
She will be true to form.

And those of the world with
Empty pockets without a coin

To judge a child on that is truly
Severe and annoying.

Or take the brown eyed beauty
All ribbons and tight curls
Should she be elevated to have a
False sense among other girls?

And that tow headed
Cute but curious boy
His parents have their hands full
But to you he's such a joy.

You may have one who steals
And maybe one who lies
Maybe there is some who
Needs hugging all the time...

But teachers teachers forget your pay
Whether great or small
And just glance around this room to see
A picture of us all.

A Show of Hands

I never saw the devil's curse
Because he could quote the book and verse
And I never saw the enemy
Because he looked just like you and me
And I never did get the name
Of the one who defeated me and came
From on high they both did you see
And both will go on eternally.
Both can do some mighty stuff
And both present miracles
Both can run a race pell-mell
But only one will lead to
And the way you know the two apart?
How to begin and where to start?
Is as close to you as where you stand
It is for them?
A show of hands.
For ones hands run smooth and show no bruise
And the one is closed to you he chooses
To with hold all good things from on high
Because you see he can't live right.
The other when he opens palms
Is wooing gently singing psalms
And within each wrist of his
Is the print of blistered sins
That he bore for all of us
Who stop our journey of wanderlust
And when we do see him for who he stands
The one thing the devil cant
Is imitate the show of hands.

Across and Up

Sometimes filling in crossword puzzles is hard
The hints are clear to the
Person who makes
The puzzles

But to the one solving it?
Well...
Different story.

The clues are a challenge at best.
I believe churches
Most of them
Are the same way
Working out one's
Place in
Ministry in
Respect in and
Even the pew we sit in
Is a challenge.
And it is we
The ones who make the puzzle that keeps people
Out.
We give them hints
And we give them clues
All of us who know the puzzle
Give them chances
To go across and up
But we
Often fail to fill in our
Own crossword puzzle game
Because you see..
We still go across
Without going up.
So while you are giving hints about who God is
And we are going across
Measuring our hints
And clues

Against each other and what each other thinks is right about the game

Well
We forget to go
Up

For in the going up
We find the solution to the puzzle.

Measuring ourselves
Our games
Hints
Clues
Motives
Attitudes
And yes even our
Choice of pew
Against the Holy Father?

Now we can begin to inch out there to the rest of the world with
A brand new
Puzzle.
And if we keep our focus on the
Up
He provides the clues
The hints
And the pew
For all.

After the Rain

It rained for days
Just came down in buckets as they say
And the levees ran high
The gutters filled
Lawns were full of mud
And the streets were slick
It poured.

Our news sent out flood warnings

He knows how it rains
He knows the ways life pours
He does.
Rains in buckets of money problems
Addictions
Lay offs
Someone out of the blue slandering
Spreading rumors
Gossip dripping and sliding filling up levees and making messes of lawns.
Kids ruining themselves with drug abuse
And
Pornography and
The gutters run full.
And yes it continues to
Rain.

But after the rain….
Flowers lift
Birds sing
Rain dries and the sky is fresh and blue and strong.
The air is sweet and there are
Clothes hanging on the line
Not lives
Not rumors
There will always be gutters and messed up lawns
But the power of light
Is always enough
After the rain.

And Maybe That's Why He Said It

God said, "No man hates his own flesh but nurtures it and tends to it."

And He said , "A man should love his wife like he loves himself."

Because he knew men would do that...
Love themselves.

Maybe that's why He said it.

And God said what a man does in secret –
In the dark, will be known at noon.

Because if it's okay to do at high noon
Then you're good to go when it's dark.

Maybe that's why He said it.

God said "Do unto others what you would have them do unto you."

Because if you can walk around in the ways you treat people? You're
still comfortable?
Walk on.....

Maybe that's why He said that too.

When God said the first shall be last and the last first
And there you are pushing to get your way to be noticed, to win and
you're so preoccupied with yourself you didn't see Him turn the line
around...

And you're nursing that black eye and smugly say "It's a man's world"
and it says so in the Bible?

God never did say that. Those are your words.

He did say "Pride comes before the fall"
So how bout' that black eye now huh?

Maybe He is trying to teach you humility
Maybe He's trying to teach you patience.
Maybe He's trying hard to get your eyes off of the natural and onto
Him the supernatural. Because the natural man is wretched, poor,
naked and blind and yes He said that too.

To rescue all of us that's why He said it.

Anything New

We wonder how in the world could Adam fall for the trick?
Then we step back and say to ourselves it was the first time.
It was the devil's first big play.
But all through the bible people fell.
They fell for the same lies the same lusts the exact same swollen pride.
Yes they did.
We cant believe the children of God:
Wandering
Begging
Staggering
Cheating
Lying
Abandoning
Shipwrecking
Tricking
Plotting
Stealing
Swearing
Ridiculing
Exaggerating
Denying
Betraying
Boasting
Pleading
Sneering
Lusting
Or
Falling.
But they did.
The sad part is:
We do the same things.

There we are at our offices, or shops our schools or clinics…our eyes
wandering, our emails begging for attention.
We stagger, and cheat and lie.
Whether its about women or taxes we are caught.

So we form
A trick
A plot
A way to steal.
To wrench free from the pain
The death that is sure to come.
Abandoning our homes
Our kids
Our spouses
We shipwreck our lives.
Swearing, denying and pleading for either the law
Or our families to not
Hold us accountable.
Then to throw everyone off

We ridicule and sneer we betray the person who got us to lust and fall in the first place.
Boasting loudly that we were perfect and that it was the other guy's fault.
Both powers shake their heads.
Neither one can believe it.
For since time began the children of God have fallen and it has never ever been over anything new.

As You Think

As you think you're going under
Go on down
Jesus is underneath you
Waiting

When you feel like going crazy
He is sane.

When you're sure you have no friends
He's there with friendship rings.

And when you think you'll
never please anyone again?

He is laughing because
He's so full of pride for you.
He's sitting on your bed ready to hug.
He's waiting just to snuggle up to you.
He will always a shoulder offer up.

And when you are so mad you want
To slap someone
Hes taken all those slaps years before.
And there are times you'd just like
To kill them all...
For thinking you a fool
And nothing more.

When you think there is no one who knows
Your heart of hearts,
And when you think that no one knows
The score,
Remember dear,
dear hurting wounded one..
That was exactly what drove the nails He bore.
He's felt the same things you have felt
And when you think that no one has...

His feet have walked ahead this same path

Remember it was those feelings that brought him to the brink
Those same curses and beatings, slashes too.
And when you get as low as you think you'll get
And you're not as alone as you think.

Because He Is Saved

Today while I was walking where my grand dad was laid
The ground was soft and there were paths that were made
By a lawnmower's cuttings a sharpened blade...
So I sat down to put flowers sat down in the shade.

And when I looked up I saw a bird
He flew up high and then would circle
I thought to myself how very absurd
To think granddad heard every word...

So if he was listening to me right then
I asked out loud if he saved had been
And I could see him lying there all boney and thin
When he walked on earth he was man among men

But did he answer my question I do not think so
For he drank and he cussed and some poker you know
And when it came for the money to show
He'd have all of it entirely to totally go...

So I asked myself well
For those things is he in?
Or does God know it all and not tell
Of how he stoops when we all fell

I remembered a time when I was just three
And grandfather sat me on top of his knee
He told me of Jesus and how to believe
So I thought to myself he's there what a relief!

But then I got worried and a little alarmed
For he was not taken to the church's arms
And actually did rebuke the preacher's charms
As he stood up for what he believed would harm.

So as I sat there on that ground paved
And continued watching the bird swing and sway
I said to myself I wont doubt or behave
That grandfathers in heaven because he is saved.

Bet You Can't

Doesn't it amaze you how Jesus did what he did?
I mean really who would do such profound miracles
And not want credit?
Why these days a man wants the credit for a loud
Burp..
Why we have become such an attention seeking society that it really
doesn't
Take a whole lot to
Pump us up.
But the Christ?
Wow.
He called men from the lowest ranks.
Smelly, sweaty, unnerving, loud and raunchy
Those fishermen had some ground to cover
To be worthy of following Christ...or did they?
The way I see it Christ knew what he was doing when He called those
twelve guys.
Took someone from every part of town.
A tax man, a doctor, a writer, a handful of sweat,
A fistful of metal, a touch of impulse
And a whole bunch of heart.
He told them to do one thing.
Follow.
Imitate.
Copy.
Simon says....

And they witnessed His healing the wounded.
The lame.
The blind.
The bleeding.
The dying.
The lonely.
And the fallen.
He never stayed around to see His performance ratings.
He never checked back to hear how well He was loved.

He was prone to feeding folks too.
He would sit in a boat,
Stand on a mount,
Walk, run and
Eventually hang just to feed us.
He never left anyone out and it didn't matter if you just ate....He'd feed
you again.

He wept too, He really did.
And it wasn't over not having a new BMW or Hummer.
It was over sin and willfulness.
It was over us and our not wanting him.

He was quick to defend the very ones we condemn
And He cast aside those we exalt.
I wish I could raise my hand or even an eyebrow without wanting
roses thrown to me...let alone Raise the dead and then say not to tell.

He chose the unlovely
Unworthy and unwanted.
He still does.
So when you get to thinkin' about that burp? And you think you're
somethin'
Cast out a demon or two
Raise the dead once or twice....I dare you
And to do it without notice?
Bet you can't.

Bibs and Pajamas with Feet

Drooling
Spitting up
Slobbering
Feeding on juice

Swallowing
Sipping
Vomiting
Burping strained fruit

Sitting up in our thrones and
Highchairs
Putting on bibs
That match the clothes
We wear.

We look way down
From our high towers
Pointing judgment and stares
Wearing baby food towels

The condemnation is served
To those we meet...
We laugh at them
Wearing pajamas with feet.

We think we are better
We are better than those
We're wearing socks and shoes
Not flannels with toes.

And then when we're home
We sit down to eat
We don't pick up a knife
To cut up our meat

We put on a drape
To catch the dribbles
Of mashed and strained grapes
We are wearing our bibs..

No difference between drooling on bibs
Covered with creamed carrots and beets
While they wear pajamas... pajamas with feet.

Blue Indigo

I thought a long time ago
When the world was just a ball
And there were animals everywhere
Right before the fall

That Christ would find great pleasure
In all His creation that day
For He created the rattlesnake
And the dangerous situation they

Create for all of us
In the country and the plains
If we are not looking closely
They strike and cause great pain

They rattle with their tails
And stir up such a fuss
They glide and slide attracting
A gathering of muck and dust

But the Lord, The Father is so wise
He knew this would not pan out
To have a dangerous snake rattling
And sneaking up throughout

So He created the blue indigo
A snake of similar size
No rattle to tell of his approach
Just opens his mouth real wide

He is the rattlesnake eater
The beauty in all blue
And without fame or fanfare
Sets upon his purpose to do

He eats the dangerous fang
And eats him tail and all
That rattlesnake devil will
Be devoured, yes he'll fall

The blue indigo will show
And he will eat him through
So will our Lord down here below
He our great indigo blue.

But They Can

I don't know why people think
They can live any ol' way they want
For years and years and years
And then drop to their knees one day
And expect God to restore them?
But they can.

The years that have been destroyed by
Bugs and drugs and locusts
To expect him to heal
They can.

Being wrong and using people
Showing no mercy and yet demanding
It from others?
Expecting it from him?
They can.

Causing the downfall of others
And having so many problems
in too deep? Thinking he'll come?
They can.

When your family has been so dysfunctional
And devastating tragedies along with so much
Bitterness?
To depend on God to fill in the blanks
They can.

I can't believe people!
They think they can just throw their cares on Him
Every single problem
And every single sin?
They can.
That He would heal their hearts
Bind up wounds
And bear sorrows?

Help them ? In spite of them?
They would not dare to dream it.
But they can.
I don't know why people think they can live any ol' way they want for years and years and years and then drop to their knees one day and expect God to forgive them and completely restore them?
But they can.

Camouflaged Christians

There are many animals
Both mammals and reptiles
That use camouflage
To protect themselves
In the wild.
They blend in
....they take
The same colors
As their surroundings.

They stay still,
Or play dead,
They sometimes
Cry out
Pretending to be wounded,
Or they'll even run.

Animals are smart.
They know that in
Order to stay alive
They have to go unnoticed,
Unsuspected,
No actions of combat,
Or rocking the boat.

And I got to
Thinking about this
The other day.
Our churches
Are full of
Christians
Much the same way.

Why, today,
This bright
Monday morning
I saw Jill Jones,

Bobby Jones'
Oldest daughter
Down at the Sweet Spot.
She was hanging out with her friends.
I walked in to grab a bite of yogurt
And heard laughter
And someone shrilly screaming,
"Jill, you little hussy what you doing touching his.....
Was he alone? Anyone see?"
And Jill in full swing of the conversation
Suddenly saw
Me
There in line.
Her voice fell out about four octaves,
And she acted
Like she'd just been hit in the stomach.

Our eyes locked and
She knew what I was thinking.
Nominated for youth group student leader..
Had spoken with her about it just yesterday at church.
She was wearing a bright pink dress and her little cross necklace.
but today?
she had cut off jeans
With gaping holes around her inner thighs...
So did the other girls....
And she blended in nicely.
Even looking real close
No one could tell she knew the Lord.

Then my mind went back to the summer of 2009.
We had rented a pontoon boat. Dan one of our deacons was the man
in charge
Leading
A group of people from our church
Along with some of his own friends from work.
Well,
We stepped onto the boat
And put our things in personal piles,

When all of a sudden one of his work buddies
Shouts out,
"Hey Jimmy where you want the brew-skies?
And the girlie – girlie maga -zeeeeens?
I told you I wouldn't forget...
Say,
Did you happen to grab my favorite from the restroom?"
And Brother Jim stopped cold like he had been hit by lightening.
blended
Stock still,
Playing dead....
All the finely mastered skills he knew.

Or how about the class reunion?
You know the one....
I went with you
Because you and I even though we graduated a year apart....
We were in the student council together.
So I am walking over to the group of women,
When I hear a woman say, "Laura, did you find a way to end the
affair?" "I mean I saw the man finally divorced that witch ....it's all over
the paper...
She's trying to take him for all he has."
"But maybe you got a piece of the action before the whole thing went
south..? Hummmmm?"
And I stood there stunned thinking to myself, "Laura, you lead the
prayer study on Tuesdays...
And afterward every Tuesday, you had your nails and hair done...I
thought it was a bit much...
And now I know where you
May have been going all along."

She looked at me
With this real wounded
Look on her face as if to
Evoke sympathy and began to cry.....
Staying safely protected behind her tender emotions...blending...
nicely....staying real safe.

Then there was the family reunion last July.
Some of the men were throwing horse shoes..others playing
Bean bag toss, and there were little clumps of folks gathered
Around tables, laughing at the food tables
And all of a sudden the music gets cranked up by someone..
And one guy hollers out to my husband..
Hey you big jerk tell us about your ol' lady...
Ooops sorry...not this old lady...you know the one I mean
Two old ladies ago...the really raunchy one who had
Your neck in a vice....

I was thinking yea...go ahead and tell us the story...
Well the thirty shades of red looked good with your red
Polo .... And come to find out you had hung onto that shirt she'd given
to you in hopes she may show up...
Wow...
Playing dead...blending in....real good at not rocking the boat
Not a force to be reckoned with and just the night before
We had prayed for our marriage to be strengthened?

You see Christ is not concerned with what you do really...as long as you
are the same...either hot or cold...blending the two gets you nowhere
but lukewarm....

Blending and staying still, pretending to be dead...not rocking the
boat...they are promises of a tomorrow...no one will notice you, bother
you, you will be accepted, liked,
Laughed with, included and promoted.
It's just such a shame isn't it
That the One who
Stood out like a rebel
And was wounded for us..
Played a tune to challenge
And change and rock all the boats of the world
Actually did die
And hung suspended
Couldn't help but notice Him
Stripped and bleeding
With laughter and plates of food

Course jokes and folks milling around
Screaming save yourself...you saved everyone else...

He just stayed still
Water blended with blood
And He fought for us

He came to stick out
Rock our world
So we could.

Cant Go Back

The old days may be full
Drinking drugging
Wine, women and song
And its purpose is clear..
It brought you to where you are.
If the old days were so phenomenal
Don't you think God in His wonderful wisdom would continue them
for your sake?
Wouldn't He want happiness for you?
Wouldn't He want you to have fun
And share laughter and good times?
Why would He choose to draw them to a close and bring you to a new
place with a memory to reflect back on the old times and wish they
were still around with the present not being happy?
Do you think God would do that?
Sure He would.
He does exactly that.
He brings us up and away from the surface where its fun and happy
and buries us deep.

Deep
Under water
In debt
In sin
With problems and
Trials.
And He keeps us there
Until we give up on the thoughts of going back.
Israel struggled with it.
They were in bondage to
Pharaoh
Moses led them out.
A couple of years into freedom they are begging for the slave drivers of
the past
Wishing for leeks and onions instead of quail.
We just can not believe how they would ever want to go back to that.
But how about us?

Drinking and drugs
Worry about paying bills or keeping secrets and turning lies into truth?
I could not imagine going back to onions and slavery. It just wasn't all that fun.
All I had was bad breath and rear view mirrors.

Cataracts

Today my husband goes for cataract eye surgery
He has been anticipating this for months
He is ready
He is excited
He is promised a new lease on life
Because he will be able to see clearly.

And the laser will correct it
The sharp as an arrow
Hot as a stove top
Accurate as a fine gauged rifle
Will be aimed to burn away the
Cataract.

I sit here and imagine what it must feel like to have cloudy vision.

And then I am
Embarrassed
For you see
I did not
See it
In
My
Own
Life.

I have cataracts
And they cloud my vision
Make me dizzy
Make my eyes strain
And give me headaches...

And I have been blaming others
All
Along.

How
Sad.

So today I place myself under Christ's laser.
His word cuts clean
Pure
Holy
And good
And chunks
Of fuzz
Blockage
And mud
Fall away.

Oh dear brother
I had cataracts
And didn't
Even know it
Because you see
I cant ever see
My own blindness
When
I
Do.

Children Aren't the Only Ones

Children lie and cheat and steal
They'll complain about a meal
And when they're mad they'll stomp and fuss
And behind a hand or under breath they'll cuss
But children aren't the only ones
They act like us.

Children are mean little dotes
Over things like
Rings and coats
And expensive things
Like cars and boats
And games to win to lose
And who has the perfect shoes...
But children aren't the only ones
They copy me and you

Children roll their eyes when they walk
They'll use poor manners
Yes they'll balk
But they're exactly like us.....
So we can't talk.

When it comes to self control what do we expect?
But perfection and respect?
But put me in the mall...
And I have none at all....
Children aren't the only ones.

Adults are grownups yes its true
But we still pick and pick and pick...
And the weak aren't struck by a truck but
By a word or two..
Children aren't the only ones they copy me and you.

So when you want to judge a kid or a child don't go too wild
When you check yourself ????
They're pretty mild.
Children aren't the only ones.

Church

What is church really
Four walls
Bathrooms
Sinks in a kitchen
And classrooms
Sounds like a
School to me
Or

Hallways that lead to two or three great big rooms
Where men give solemn talks
And the are flowers and visiting rooms too.
Sounds like a
Mortuary
To me
Or
Spacious places to shoot hoops
And a track to run on
And coffee shops
With an espresso machine
And sauna.
Now that sounds like my workout gym
Rows and rows of seats
Layered for people to sit and
Look over a bigger room
Where they can feel a part of the action and get noticed for being
there.
Sounds like a stadium
To me.
Or
A huge facility with games and singing and bands
And food and people taking risks
With their money and their futures
Colorful carpets and plush
Expensive chairs.
Sound like a casino.
So how about it

Friend?
What is church to you?
Because I can sing
Jesus loves me
All I want
At home.

Close

I guess Mr. Hankston had put down that ol'bottle and picked it back up again a million times in 65 years.

He'd been struggling with that demon since he was a teen. And he sat there on the far side of 60 just watching every face in the place. Young old fat rich skinny ugly or poor never mind all that he was intently staring each and every soul in the eyes.

He had a wife. He had had three. And he had had a family too...but they were gone.

Been gone nigh 35 years now too. And he sat there listening to the other couples discuss their highs and lows and he felt far away. Far far far away. He often drifted into thought. Such deep far out places he'd go; it was almost like a real trip with him leaving in a Car and always his wife would ask "Where are you now?"

He wouldn't answer but just nod like he agreed when all the time she hadn't asked for agreement at all.

Sometimes around the eleven or twelve he would come around ..sneak up on her a peck her cheek lightly..bid her good night and go to bed. There in the rectangle of terror he would dream.

This is what he dreamed
Every night the same.
Surrounded by water and boats and life jackets and buoys every size every shape in all capacities able to save....but he would not reach for one.

He kept on swimming and treading water not getting' anywhere and getting tired and more tired by the minute. His wife would be on shore waving to him with a white handkerchief as if to say give up cling to one of the life saving devices and get on shore with me....but the water was warm and the comfortable and the shore looked hot with the sun bearing down....he'd swim a little and flip on his back blow a couple of fountains with his mouth... and life would go on.

He'd wake up and life was the same.....
Until one night he was about to go to bed when he decided to have a drink.
He swigged down a shot or two of brandy

And went to bed...that night was no different...same water same shore same same same.......

But this time he saw a man walking toward him in his dream. He tried to open his eyes but he could not ...and he recognized Jesus.. Mainly from shows or movies,,it was..the odd thing about dreams is that people can be different entities and you still fully know what they or who they are. And this Jesus was a child. Standing there in a little t-shirt and shorts she was holding out her hand with a pair of water wings in them as if to say "If I could do it couldn't a grown man such as yourself come too?" And he looked the child in the eyes and smiled but the child did not smile she just determinedly held out the slip on wings. He came close to taking them that night.

But the next night the same child was there holding out water wings again. Come on she motioned with her little lips come on you are so close...so so so close.

This went on for weeks until finally in his sleep one night she turned her back to walk away. Nooooooo! he screamed out ....Noooooooo! and his wife stirred and he woke.
What a nightmare she said. What did you dream? I came close to the shore...came close to where you are..
Close?
Yes close.
That Sunday the pastor and his wife came over to call.
At the door Mr. Hankston about fainted.
He did not even hear the explanation of why the child was with them..didn't hear a thing about not having a sitter at the last minute

But when that little girl came through the door he bent down and said "I'm close".
"I know" she said close is not going to carry you...you could use these...and from behind her back she produced some water wings... oh Sarah ...please forgive us she doesn't know what she is doing...
Not so thought Mr. Hankston
But

Close.....
And now ?

He dreamed that night the same
But the girl? The wings?
He grabbed on and ended up on the shore.

Did You?

You didn't think that God would be that small
Did you?
To let you think He wasn't real
And get away with it?

You didn't actually think
Muslims and
Buddhists and
Hindus
Were on speaking terms with God
Did you?

You didn't really believe that God just
Spun the world around like
A top
Turned His back
And let us spin
And spin....
Did you?

I can't imagine someone of your
Intelligence really
Thinking
No actually believing that
You had the ability to
Become a God like
Our holy One...
Or
Did you?

I, for the life of me can not
See you really believing that kind of lie
That kind of false delusional thinking...
Because you surely knew that if we
Were capable of becoming Gods
Then what
Would happen

On the
Six o clock news?
I bet you didn't think of that now …
Did you?

I know for me
I could never be even close to the same…as God
You couldn't either
Because you knew just keeping your temper from
Boiling is hard
Hard enough
Let alone be
God

To have the power to cause thunder and
Lightning to crash and
Fall from the sky?

To cause the mating seasons and the growing
Seasons and heck just the four seasons.…
You haven't tried that yet or
Did you?

Did you succeed?
No?
But when you
Leaned on Him
You found favor
And refuge
Peace
and joy
And love
I knew you would.

Dollars and Sense

There were times in my life when I've had plenty
There have been times I've gone without
I know what it is to be broke and well fed
Therefore I find contentment in all positions
Hungry
Or full
Naked or clothed
I know I can control
All things through Christ who strengthens me.

That is not how the verse goes.

We get far too used to controlling
Tallying
Adding in
Subtracting out
Keeping receipts
Keeping bills
Shredding documents
Licking stamps
Installing software
Deleting accounts
Putting this aside keeping change jars
Clipping coupons
Adjusting thermometers
Taking this outfit back
Wearing shoes for another year
Used dishes
Garage sales
Second job
Mortgages too
Wine

Dine
Entertain
Eat out
Eating at
Everything costs money
So tell me which of those things do you control?

If It Weren't for a Merciful Lord
Not one penny would be worth a
Nickel.
Nothing saved would count..
Banks can close, tumble and crash.
You simply do not have the power to tell God how to run the show.
He doesn't want your scrawny help
Isn't staying up all night waiting for your suggestions
And he could care less how you feel about it either.
He is in control.
Not you
So tell me can you by worrying
Change one hair black or white?
Because at the end of it all that my friend is what you will have:
A head full of gray hair.
By the way that scripture is correct.

Don't Even Look

When a person chances to open
To open the book
And they read a few scriptures
And they see all the crooks
And all of the losers and all the sin too
Well they think it's no big deal
For them to do the same to you
And they puff out their chests and
Walk around tall
And they act like they haven't any brains
At all...
And so I have to take them to Matthew the book
And prompt them to read there yes
Take a look

When it talks about murder and treating your
Brother
We aren't to even hate or slander each
Other...
And when the bible talks about divorce
And oaths too
Let your yes be yes and our no's be
True....
And you heard it was said in the Old Testament
Books
Eye for an eye
Don't believe me then
Look
And if your habit offends you then cut the thing out
It'd be better to go around armless than
From fire shout.
And if you're confused about how much you should give
Give till it hurts and then he said that will be when you live.
As for praying and paying your tithe
If you do to be seen
All you're showing is pride
And if you pray out loud and in public carry on

You can rest assured people around you are turned off
They will think you are wrong.
So when a man sees a member of the opposite sex.
He dare not look long he won't be blessed
For the hate and the slander you do in your heart
Is done in your body
You just don't' know you have
Started.
So when you can't stand it and can't read this old book
Remember to start with the simple stuff
And don't even look.

Drawing Lines

A teacher was standing afar
Watching a little boy drawing a car
And there in the desk behind his too
A girl dressed in pink was drawing **you**
As the teacher walked by she knew
What his was
It was a car flinging up dust.
But for the girl she stood and stared
For she had not a clue and she knew that
She dared
Not to ask
So as she walked from child to child
She noticed drawings of castles and wild
Animals with some from farms
And she saw some drawings of monsters
Quite alarmed.
And as she began to circle back through
She only saw a single line drawn in light colored blue
The girl had spent twenty minutes or so
Making certain the line was straight you know
And so the teacher stirred the courage to ask
What was the line for? Before she walked past.
This is the lord said the girl without fear
And the next time you look the line will
Be nearer.
You understand God don't you Mrs. Knight?
He does not have to put up a fight.
He just lays down a line and stands on it
And for those who stand with him
The fight is over the enemy quits.
For you see now surely you do
The lord will come for us out of blue
And he will come right on time
For all of those who crossed his line.
And for the ones who stood on it instead?
Dear teacher of mine he'll raise from the dead.
So yes even though my picture is plain

I know that my God will come again
And this line you see dividing this page?
Well that's whats to happen in the coming age.
The blue line will certainly be torn
And the whole world will hear a rams horn
And wherever you are you will fall to your knee
And you will no doubt about cry "Thou art holy"
Angels and demons have fought through the ages
For mankind to follow through life's various stages
And we chosen one or both and the same
Either God who is holy or the enemy's flame.
I know my picture of God is small
But don't be surprised by it at all
He is magnificent and he is truth
And I am standing on this line so now teacher are you?
The teacher was extremely surprised to see this girl be so wise
But she said "Just add a sunset to your line of blue"
And you know she did not know how right she was.
Because the time is so near the line coming closer to each of us
And so the girl picked up her crayon of black
And added a cloud or two way in the back.
So when the teacher walked by once again she
Did not smile but frowned once again.
"Now you know I asked you to draw a sunset to go with the blue"
"Ah but" the little girl said
It doesn't matter you are already dead.
"What ?!" The teacher was noticeably hurt
to hear such judgment From this little squirt.
And she took up the picture and threw it away
Then told the class to go outside to play.
But when the kids were all outside
She took out the drawing and in her notebook she'd hide
And the next Sunday as she was in church
The preacher was speaking about leaving this earth
And He said "You may be feeling just fine but don't ever be bold
enough to cross that blue line."

The teacher slightly gasped as reached for the drawing
And the next thing she knew she was kneeling and bawling
She repented of her sins that day and time
She knew she was standing with the girl on the blue line!

Drive Through Christianity

Can you see how far we have progressed?
Doesn't it just baffle your mind?
We have everything bite sized
Compact and mid-drifted.
I cant believe we actually still park our cars and come in to sit for a
church service!
I mean really how archaic!
There should be a window for us to swing in and order…
Maybe it would look and sound something like this:

"I'll take a short scripture and medium sized prayer and throw in a
second verse of 'Just as I Am'"
Or
"Ya know I'm in a hurry don't have time for the combo just give me the
main scripture and I'm outta here."
Or
"I've had a hard week I think I will have you super-size the whole order
and throw in a fourth verse to 'my anchor holds' I'll finish the meal off
with a dose of grape juice for extra precaution.
Or maybe you are like the last guy…
"better hold the praying and hold off on the singing y'all aren't nothing
but a bunch of hypocrites going to hell faster than anyone so for me
today …I guess I'll just skip right to faith without works is dead and
yep ill only come to this restaurant when you preach what I want to
hear…you know feed me something I can really sink my teeth into…"
How sad
I hear our father say.

Everlasting water and the bread of life available at every meal.…
and they're still looking in their rear view mirrors to check their
lipstick.

Everyone Has a Couch

Red taillights backing up
Traffic slowing down
We radioed ahead
And
That young man
Never knew what happened.
That couch ...
That couch...
Fell off
The back of a pickup
In the dark
Going so fast
He never saw it.
Hit it on his bike.
But it saw him
And it
Killed him.
And you know?
Everyone has
A couch.

Everyone has something
That hits
Em' real hard
And it tries
To them....

So in your life
Think about
Potential couches
It may be a poor
Childhood or
Disease
Or
Hate
Or
Ignorance

Or intolerance
Some other
Life stealing
Breath shortening
Joy killing
Demon
But if you understand
That
Couches
Fall
All
The time
And you don't have to die
You can
Survive
And not just survive
But excel
And grow stronger
And prosper even
Then you can allow for the falling of
Couches.
Because
Couches?
Well couches are
Also used by friends to sit on
And share a bowl of popcorn.

Exhausted

My sister lay on her back
She'd just run around the track
Around and around and around again
Hoping with the fourth lap....a win!

And the newspaper clipping that I have
Makes me happy, yes I am glad
That it was her and not me there
With wringing wet clothes and messed up hair

And the practice the training and long hours
Of preparing for that race without flowers
Arrests my thoughts and captures attention
For back in 1985 she was mentioned

And then just the other day
Her daughter in the news was playing
She was in an athletic hall
Playing an intense match of volleyball

And it struck me then again hard
Both young women with no holds barred
Both ran and trained with their teams
And both on shelves their trophies gleam.

But when I think of the race in life
And my sis has a family and she's a wife
Does she remember back to that day
When she lay exhausted from the race?

For this life sometimes has me beat
And I lay down with aching feet
I could do better at the race than this
If I would train and practice like my sis

And at the finish line would be my friends
And the Christ the Lord announce my win.
And I know the outcome be applauded
Even though I'd fall exhausted.

Fleas Lice and Maggots

Fleas can live on anything unclean...
Like dogs
Or cats
Or even
On the human
Scalp
They thrive on
Stimulation.
So the more a person vacuums them up
The more they will
Reproduce.
A good washing usually cures the problem.
Lice?
Now there's a different story.
Lice live and feed on the
Dead.
They will not disappear with a wash.
They must have their source of air cut off
Yes they have to be suffocated to get rid of lice.
But my brother if you have maggots?
There is a problem.
Maggots consume feed on and host on the
Dead
And you know?
We all suffer with some form of
Flea
Lice
Or maggot sin problem.
Sin is just that way.
It is either jumping around feeding on unclean jokes or nasty thoughts
or maybe bugging us with perverse motives.
And sometimes a person has a lice
Sin problem.
You know what I mean...
Addictions and habits that are out of line with the will and heart
of God.

But cutting off the source of air to that old guy will be the only way to get rid of the sin-lice.

But oh dear christian..

If there are hosts of sin-maggots?

Think of it this way..

You

Don't

Feel

Any prick in your conscience.

You are not just outside of God's will for your life anymore....

No, my friend if you have maggots?

You're dead.

Flies

The flies from six houses got together for tea
They discussed the situations in their houses you see
And the first fly is speaking at this moment..currently..

My house is a rambling sort of collage.
It begins with steeple rooftops and ends with garage..
And within the rooms there only lives four.
Two kids and a dad (the mother's a bore)
And what happened this week I'll tell you for sure
Had me awake all night long thinking and staring
For the teenager kept his stereo blaring
And the bored woman of the house was screaming
"I'm outta here you are all worthless...I'm leaving!"
The man did not flinch he'd heard worse I guess
And the youngest the girl was just getting dressed.
She ran to the mother threw her arms around her
And said "oh no not now I'd be lonely for sure."
Well at that minute the dad took control and he started a
Ruckus that would make you find a hole..
But he was blocking the doors off from leaving
And by now the poor woman's chest it was heaving
The stereo continued to blast away
And the whole thing brought tears of remorse and dismay
To my little fly eyes for in that hour
I realized just how much they have power
To create a tone either warm or not
And they all contribute with whatever they've got..

Well said fly number two
That's nothing compared to what I'll share with you..
This morning right after breakfast this was heard..
The firing of a gun and the killing of birds.
What the other flies said together
This is so strange it doesn't make sense whatsoever
And that is when the third fly chimed in and he said yep I had to go
over there and protect my fly friend...what you were over there in the
same home?

"Wow" said the other three "How did it turn out?"
We pretended to fly real angrily
And with no fear we zapped him you see.
For had we not bit him and flown to his face
he may have slung the weapon at his wife's little face.
See she was all pitiful there on the couch and complaining and griping
about his going out and he took his anger out on those birds
But we distracted him to try to save her.
And then the other two flies agreed their stories were nothing
compared to these..
And the moral was this among flies
You never know what happens you'd be surprised..
For the homes one would think are the happiest
Are those filled the worst unsettled distress.
So watch what you say and of course what you do...
for you never can tell a fly may be watching you.

Following

There are things that follow.
Things like tails and curtains after a performance and clapping too---
Yes, those are things that follow.
Some think following is bad. It's because if
You're not leading well ---
You're following
Which must mean you're slower
Or maybe not smart enough to lead.
Sometimes following is a good thing though.
Like following a chocolate chunk cookie
With a glass of milk
Or a handshake with a hug
Or a job well done with a pat on the back.
We that follow Christ follow him to eternity.
and yet most of us have a past following us.
A pervasive, nasty, offending odor following.
And so it goes we follow Christ but our past follows us...so
Christ, out of the corner of his eye
Sees that thing cinching up our shoulders,
Tagging around our hips
Clamping onto our throats
With a long and steady stare he brings that past
To the cross. Because you see that is where..
That is the spot where our past can not follow.
Remind yourself of that the next time your past follows you around
like
A stinky dead maggot filled skunk
Leave it there and walk away.
Don't look back. There's no need ..nope .No one's following. Leave it at
the foot of the cross and walk away...

Frogs

The scientist grabbed up an
Unsuspecting frog
Plopped him in a pot with
The water sloshing it
Reminds the little guy of home
Snug and close
Wet and warm.
The scientist turns
A knob on the stove
The pot heats up.
Little bubbles rise up from
The bottom
And the frog swims less
And floats more.
Fairly soon the water
Boils and the amphibian
Doesn't move at all.
He is thrown into the garbage.
The scientist goes to neighborhoods
And slings teenagers into
Pots turns up the heat
And kills em' all
Arms and legs brimming.
Trash cans full .
Goes to get the next one
Turns the knob to 'high.'
But a shadow falls across the man and the stove is turned to 'off'.
He is picked up by his coat collar and thrown into a lake.
Gradually heated?
No
It is a
Burning lake of fire.
And you know?
The banks are covered with frogs lookin' on.

From a Distance

From a distance
From half way around the world
The man sat in a chair
In the office
Somewhere in the Turkey
And gives me advice
About a computer I did not create
A computer I do not understand
A computer I would throw out the window
If not for his patience.
And I follow his instructions exactly and I cant see him and
I have never met him face to face
Eye ball to eye ball.

But still if he says click on here or there
I do
And when he says shut this down and boot this up
I do
And we get off the phone..
And I sit here and
It washes over me
I don't even trust God that much...
Why some mere man has more
Influence than God?
And me
I end up
Trusting a
Computer
Guy.

From Now On

"From now on" said the mom
"I will be monitoring your coming in times
And your going times…"
"I will know who you are with at every moment and what you are
doing."
"If you are at a movie"
"Well, from now on I will likely pop up out of no where to make sure
you are there."
"I will have black teeth and sweat pants on with a nasty dingy shirt to
prove to you that from now on you are not getting by with anything."
"I will not cut you any slack and I will not listen to any excuses."
"From now on you are going to be accountable and reliable and
responsible and dependable and you best be ready with a definite
answer if I ask you a question."
"From now on your friends will be questioned and your bedroom,
books and all private time will be timed."

After this long speech the mom waited for her son to reply.
Several minutes passed and the teenager looked his mother right in
the eyes and said…

From now on you have no worries, no concerns about my times books
or friends. You have no reason for any explanations or excuses and you
are right you wont have to cut me any slack or have to listen to me.
And he turned from her went to his room and after a few moments he
opened the door and tacked his schedule on the door.

It read:
"At precisely 8:00 tonight I am going out I will be coming home at
exactly 8:01. From now on.
"Good" thought the mother.
And at eight pm she heard the gun.

From now on we'll choose our battles
From now on we'll trust God more.
From now on we'll say no to being control freaks.

From now on we as parents will guide while we lead and lead with our lives. Live with our words and use our words to validate our walk.

Then the mom would say:

From now on I will trust you until you prove me wrong.
I will gladly meet your buddies and invite them over. I will never embarrass you surprise you or intimidate you because you are worthy of my respect and you are worthy of your space and you are entitled to privacy. Should something happen beyond your control that keeps you from being on time I will listen and I will try to understand. From now on you are free to be yourself and when you are frightened or confused you can come to me for advice or money or my extra support.

The teen turned to his mother and said
"From now on you have no worries, no concerns about my times books or friends. You have no reason for any explanations or excuses and you are right you wont have to cut me any slack or have to listen to me.
And he turned from her went to his room and after a few moments he opened the door and tacked his schedule on the door .

"At precisely 8:00 tonight I will be going out."
"At precisely 8:01 pm. I will be coming home"
"Good" thought the mom
And at eight pm. She heard his bedroom door close and the CD she had given him for Christmas banging out a tune..."hey mom!" He yelled "Come on in I want you to hear this...from now on."

Good People Are the Worst

If you ever check up and down the pews
And if you're ever wondering who's spreading Good News
And if you left it up to me so that I could pick and choose?
I say good people are the worst.

They are the worst at forgiveness because
They've never "done it"
Terrible at extending grace because they can't even comment
And when it comes to being saved? And all the joy to share?
They sit way back They simply don't care.

And so you say why do they come to service every Sunday?
Especially if they are not about to follow through on Monday?
All I can say is that I know they sit under a Curse...
And to get them to do anything? Well good people are the worst.

They drive RV's
And watch big screen T.V.'s
And have a thirst for knowledge and power
But to show the strength in a midnight hour

You see they are all about the mirror if you <u>will</u>
And how their hair flips up just right ...and they peer ..**Until**
The preacher gets too close to home and the blinders come flying off
That's when they look away and softly and daintily cough
"Oh no not me" is what they say
"I don't know how to brighten anyone's day"
"No kidding" I'm wanting to burst
Because you're a good person? '
You are the worst.

GPS

My son used a friends GPS to find the route to a place he had never been before. He punched in the address and bam! This little map popped up on the screen and from where they were it highlighted the complete route and distance and estimated time it would take for the complete trip. He reached the destination easily and on time with no stressful u turns and guess and check entry ramps.

I thought to myself why cant life the christian life be like that? Just punch in "heaven" and have your estimated life span pop up and your path highlighted with the exact roads and turns to take to reach the anticipated destination safely and on time.

God just does not operate that way. He wants us to lean on him and sometimes taking a wrong turn here and there teaches us to trust him even more. If we knew how long we would live I'm sure some of us would give up and some wouldn't even get out of bed. There would be some people who would overpower the entire world just due to their knowing how long they would live. There would also be some who if they lived as long as they found they were going to? Well a homeless guy may just quit. So this is the way I see it. We have this map. Called the bible and inside is the way to get where we want to go. In this book there are examples of folks who did not do such a great job following the path and we can read about their consequences. There are others who have followed and lost their way or have taken detours and yet because of faith they made it and they set an example too. So don't expect man to ever discover or uncover or recover a fool proof, exactly perfect instrument to get him to heaven. Remember not everyone wants to go there anyway, they surely mustn't because the GPS has been around for a long, long time.

He Can Surely Use Us

There's Adam and eve
Whom satan deceived
And the first kid's name
Was Cain

There was Noah the ark
And the 40 days embarked
And with him his daughters in law did lay

There is Samson with hair
And Daniel I swear
With those lions it is true
And what about Gideon
And it's all about Midian
And the ones lapping
Were through

With Jacob who lied
And Esau who tried
To kill his younger brother
And lived
It was only because
Our father above
Led Esau to truly forgive

Then with Joseph's bragging
And Moses' swaggering
And banging the rod on a rock
The man of God
Rode on the donkey
And actually heard the thing talk!

And what about Saul
Should have killed them all
But Samuel heard the sheep
Talk dying
What about lots wife trying

To be a salt shaker asleep!

Abraham wandered and lied
And his beautiful wife
Said to say she was his sister
He did and was caught
Did not do as he ought
No he should never have listened

There's the three guys who walked
And the fourth one who talked
With them in that hot fire
Elijah too
Had a chance before noon
To show that our God is no liar

We can't forget the kings
And how Esther brings
Her beauty to the throne
And can't cast aside
David's heart full of pride
But look at the psalms that he wrote!

Depression, disease
Death, misery
All had their holds on these men
But God used them still
Wouldn't give up until
They were brought into heaven

And just that much
Doesn't even touch
The new testament books
With so much more
Than has been talked
About for sure
Open them up take a look

For surely you see

They're no different
From me
Between all of them we've discussed
But if God used them then
He can use we weak men
Yes
He can surely use us!

He Was Already There

That would be a night Peter would never forget…
Boat about to splinter
Storm raging around him like a cougar
And the wind!
Some of the men were wailing and some were praying.
But when he saw the Christ there in the wind and the waves
Welcoming him to step out and walk with Him on the water?
He did.
For a moment in time faith was held suspended between moon and
dashing wave.
But he sank
And when he did, Jesus lifted him up again.
He was already there.

Those three would not bow down
The furnace was lit seven times hotter and even then
It was no match for the king's fury..
Throw them in!
Down
Down
Down
They fell
Until they landed on the platform where the king could watch them
die.
But wait!
Did we throw three or four men in?
For it is reported there were four men walking around in the fire..
And the fourth one looked like the son of man
Because you see Christ was already there too.

He was there in that royal courtroom to see the scepter raise in
Esther's presence.
There in the den petting lions too..
He was in the bush blazing with holiness watching Moses with eyes as
big as plates,
He was in the tomb with Lazarus and in the fire that fell from heaven
called down by old Elijah

He was already there in the ark helping Noah with all those animals.

So when you face storms of gossip or raging seas of mistakes, take
heart He's there.
And when you just know that the fire could not be any hotter?
The family you try to be welcomed into just might not?
Maybe you are sure you have been thrown to the lions and quite
possibly are stuck deader than Lazarus in a tomb you've been living so
wrong.
Maybe you believe if you had to corral another kid it would be just like
gathering animals onto an ark?
Well He's there.
He has gone into tomorrow
Has seen yesterday,
Knows the end of the story.
So don't quit
Don't slow down
Don't even think about falling
Because He's there
He's already there.

How

How can I sit
In a
Seat
Of
Judgment
Against
You?

Since when did I
Become so
Strong
So
Very perfect?

How do I stand
In the place
Of condemnation
While
You
Wriggle and squirm
Under
My microscope?

Since when did I
Become so close to the
Trinity
That they call it a
Quartet?

How can I crawl to
Where you
Are?
Because I
I am
Not that big.

Not big enough
To hang for you
And not strong enough
To rise
Again for
You.
And it won't be me
Coming in
The
Clouds
For your
Soul.

So I will
Forgive you
I must
For you see
I will need
It
Next.

I Am All

There was Adam, he lied
And Moses ran,
Abraham did both,
So did Samson and

What about Jacob
What did he do?
His name meant liar
God changed it, had to!

The way he swindled and tricked his brother?
And even incorporated the help of his mother?

And then there was Joseph
And Elijah, those men..
Were always in trouble
Back in the old testament

There were the three in the furnace until there were four
And they were saved because of the Lord...

There was Daniel and Jeremiah two honorable guys
But would have never accomplished anything in their own eyes

If it weren't for the Holy host of heaven
No, none of these people were at all any better.

Then take Saul and David they both were a trip
Neither one could tell the truth worth a solid lick.

On and on and down through the ages
We read of liars and thieves and loud mouthed rages...

And the thing I see the common thread
Is that I am them all
I know in my head

That I have been a Moses
And singing David
I have run like Jacob
And a lying Abram

I have tricked like Jacob, thrown fits like Saul
And I have been found on my knees.. gone there to bawl.

I have been a Daniel too
And wept like
Old Jeremiah
Morning and noon.

I have missed the Lord so many times
And yet He has found me and healed me in spite...

Of all my mistakes and my poor decisions
But without doubt
When I die I'll see him

And even though I sin
And totally fall
A new thing for God?
No I am all.

I Beat You

"I beat you mommy" he said at three
With a pack of cards showing rummy

"I beat you son" She yelled right back
When he played the six with she the jack

And then again at sixteen years
He fussed and cussed and punched her ears

So that when she recovered her ground
She called police and had him found.

Nothing was said between them then
And the distance went from thick to thin

Until one day he showed at her door
A strapping man of thirty four

And they sat down at the table
To talk and play some cards if they were able

To regain the years they had lost
And the love the bridges they had to cross.

And when they both saw time was fleeting
They both agree to cease from beating.

For the little boy who began at three
Had now been the one getting beat.

And the mom too saw the light
That being the one to win is not always right.

And so the mom turned to her son
And said "Please let me be the one"

Who runs to you as fast as I can
To restore the love and understand...

That I will gain such joy yes a treat too
If in that game that race I will beat you.

I Can Fly

The mother sat in that jail cell holding her hands up to her face. She squinted at the purple veins under her skin. How long had she had those? They looked like lumpy green beans under there.

Just then she looked up and saw a girl at the door with a guard. He was shaking his head as he opened the jail door and the girl said "Mom let's go home".

In the car the mom said
"I can fly ya know".
Her daughter said nothing.
Again the mom said
"I can fly"
"Sure you can fly mom, but can you land?"
"Can you land mom?"
"Can you land?"

Two weeks later the mom sober now sitting on the couch eating a sandwich..
"I *can* fly you know " She said
The girl whirled around
"Mom you can not fly!"
"Some glad morning when this life is over I'll fly away" the mom sang softly.
"Will you fly too?"
"Yes, mom I will fly too"
She gave her mother a hug. A month later her mother passed away. And as the girl straightened her mother's bed she saw a handful of white feathers....probably from her mother's pillow.
But she never did shake the fact that her mom knew how to fly and left those feathers to prove it.

I Had Them Too

I had a dream I wanted to be
A doctor to go across the seas

To give to them in Jesus' name
One who would go treat them all the same...

But that door was shut as tight as a drum
And I gave up a sigh and wanted to run

Then I had misery and a struggling life
Didn't understand and I broke down and cried

I worked hard but no matter the plan
I 'd end up misunderstood by myself I would stand.

Then my son came to me and said I'm going to go
I wanted to be able to reach out and touch him though

He said he needed to leave to find his mission in life
And so once more did I receive a dagger and knife to my side.

With these three things I ran to you
Said what more can I take? "what more should I do?

What more is there to life for me I don't know
And when you opened your mouth your blessings did pour.

First of all I was the doctor and still am ...He said
I bind up wounds and raise people from death.

But as far as being recognized?
For the healing and the sacrifice?

I had a dream that all would be healed...
But rather than that they wanted me killed

And as for your life of struggling misery?
I had one too ...remember Calvary?

So when to me your heart do pour
Remind yourself I was there before.

And as for the last part the mission of your son?
I get that too because I have just one

The only difference between me and you
Is that you used to have dreams and I still do.

Dreams to prosper you to further your faith
Broaden your area to make you great.

So get up in my strength and fight to pursue
Those wont get you down because I have them too.

I Have Something in My Eye

I have something in my eye
And it is bothering me
It cant be very big
But no matter what the size may be
I have something in my eye and
I can barely see
But even though I have some little hair
I can help you with your problems
That I see there

Let me pick them out for you
So we can share
First let me start with your kids
And from where I sit and
Stand
I cant believe or imagine and
The ways you've let them run and they
Ran....
I feel certain that the next
Issue
Is your marriage
Yes grab a tissue
And how much your husband
Missed you
When
(and it is from my point of view)
You abandoned him and your kids
Too.
What I wish to correct
Next
Is your messy disorganized
Closets
And the entire house is a total
Mess!
I see the dirt lying
Everywhere
And its plain to see you just don't

Care
Why I see clothes piled up
Everywhere
Covering the couch and the
Chairs.
And next the topic is your choice of
Friends
(this is where my patience ends)
From what I can see
(and it all depends)
On how strong a message your marriage
Sends
Yes my eye is hurting like mad
And the vision in it is getting bad
But watching your problems makes me sad
To see you turn out like
That.
I was just at the doctor
Have God to thank
For He saw my eye before I
Tanked
And surely He played a
Prank...
To say there is in my eye
A two foot
Plank..

I Just Did Not Believe You

I kept it up until she was gone
You could hear the man say
And then turned to his counselor
And buried his head to pray..
I never thought she would
Have enough
He sobbed into his hands
And to watch the happiness
Shes robbed
Leaves me desperate and mad

Now wait said his mentor
His counselor and friend
Did she give fair warning before her patience
Neared the end?
The man sat up real still
And looked him square in the eye
She said it a million times doc
Before she said "goodbye"..
And what would you do when she would
Say those things from out of the blue?
The man slowly lifted up
His head and voiced the words
I don't believe you
Well then said the doctor
This is where you must begin
If you still love her then
It will all depend...
On the next four days
Maybe five
Said the doctor slowly
You have to find a way to prove to her
You're holy.

Day one
Dear diary the man neatly wrote
Help me if you can

I am just an middle aged and semi balding
Man
But I have to find a way to prove to my ex-wife…
That she is my treasure and the center of my life.
So today dear diary I will phone her up
And I will woo her gently through my voice
I'll call her bluff

Ring! Ring! the telephone rang four more times or more
Before a lady's voice said
"Hello?" and then listened to be sure
Uh honey the man said into the receiver
I am a mess without you here he'd make her
A believer..
Oh yea she shouted into the phone
On the other end?
You are not a man upon anyone can depend
You are not one bit holy Godly or refined
And to go back with you
Would be a lose
Do you think I am that blind?
The man swallowed real real
Hard and tried to find his voice..
But she hung up
And the next thing he knew
He found she'd made her choice.

Day two
Dear diary that yesterdays call
Why it was such a flop!
It took my ego and my spirit and
A pin to a balloon it popped.
I think I will read the chapter in
The book of psalms..
What to do when someone wrongs you
How not to take it wrong..
So he looked up a chapter and read it right
Out loud..but that day he was afraid
Just the birds were his crowd.

After reading he paused to pray
Just a simple prayer
And asked God for her to talk again
Please let me know she cares
He stared at the phone
But it lay silent and for a minute said
He
I will not call her no I wont
But how will she believe?

So he picked up the phone on day two
Of he and his mentors plan
And when she picked up he said
Real fast I'm
Just an ordinary man
I just want a moment to tell you dear
Of my morning quiet time
How I have been a real big jerk
And confused and so so blind!
She said well you are right about
It all and I don't have the time
To find out right now if you are really
Lying.

She hung up the phone again that day
She hung up on him hard
And when he turned around
His face was clouded in parts
Dear God he whispered
What have I done?
To make her this mad at me
And what can I do
To make her see
I getting close to you?

Dear diary day three is here and
Nothing more is new..
But only that I have a plan
To make her believe me too

He called her up one more time and sweetly and
Gently said …
I long to hold you in my
Arms
And offer my lap to lay your head
She heaved out a sigh and
Let it go and said into the phone
You are a nice man of course but please
Leave me alone…
Oh no I cant he said real fast
And don't hang up again
I have to know how I can
Change your mind and
At least become your friend
Well when you prepare me
Ten verses to a song
That already has twenty?
Then I'll forget your wrong.
And when you can make the
Flowers all around my house
All my favorite color?
I wont think you're a louse
And when you spend five minutes
Lifting up the poor
And spend at least ten more
Giving without it being such
A chore?
And when the preacher says you have
Been in church
For more than a
Sunday or two…
But attend and give tithe and
Offerings
Then I will believe in you.

Day four he was so busy looking for a song
That boasts of twenty verses
Boy oh boy that's long!
But her finally found a love song from the olden

Days in Russia
And then he sneaked over at lunch and replanted
The flowers with his
He gave to charity that day
And began attending functions
He paused every few moments to pray
And let the holy spirit unction

And then he called her on the phone
Fourth day in a row..
He said into the piece
Go look outside I have you something to show.
She went and while she was
Walking her sang her the Russian song..
But she broke down a wept
So he cut it out not to make it
That long....
That was the song that my grandfather
Played to my dear grandmother
And whats more that is for sure
My families theme song unlike all
Others.
How did you know she tearfully wept?
What made you choose that out of
The blue?
He said into the phone
Real slow
I just did not believe you!
The two got back together and stayed together for life
.he the doting husband and
She the beautiful wife..
And when upon the visit to the doctor
He took his new bride too
To give report on progress
She knew what she had to do
Said she when she met the man
Who had challenged her husband dear
He must have had the truth of God
Put clean through him..hear?

For now he is just as perfect and
As precious as he can be...
And you can rest sound and
Assured
He's made a believer out of me...

I Know You Said

I know you said my burden is light but why is my life so heavy?
And when you said you were the way the truth and the life well .. I lose
my way and lie about it all the time.
When you said all that stuff about forsaking this world for heaven
I guess I really didn't believe you or I'd have never bought that second
Cadillac when the Dodge was running just fine..
The time you said not to repay evil for evil?
I just had to give that boss man his due.
I know what you said about not lustfully staring or purposefully hating
and I fail miserably on both accounts.
When you said not to store up wrath ... I take an abundance of
contemptible anger into my hands and push it into my heart and store
it there.
I know you said I'd never thirst if I drank living water and I could fight
the devil with your word and win...
But I die of thirst every single day and run at the first sign of trouble.
You said a lot about humility and pride and I walk around falsely with
large amounts of both..
I repeatedly cause you to wonder if I have ever read your word at all.
I have forsaken every commandment, every rule, law and suggestion
You have ever made.
I have walked
Talked
And sang in my own strength.
I would have healed in it too if I could.
I have carried guilt
Envy
And sorrow all over the
Wrong things and never showed them towards the things or the
people
I should have.
I know you said I was dust.
But I knew you meant mountain...
I knew you said not to lean on my own wisdom but I
Figured
You were kidding.
I know you said to be patient

To watch my mouth
And hold my tongue…
To not do good deeds before men..
But I run and push to be the first..
To open my mouth
About myself
And what I
Have
Done….

But
You also said
My grace is sufficient
My blood covers all sin
And it is finished…I know

Yes I know you said that too.
And you said
The first will be last and the last first..
After all…
I have fallen short on, been found lacking in and yes come last for
every single race..
So..
Maybe there is still hope.

I Saw a Cat

The other night in my sleep----

I saw a cat.

Skinny, little thing.

Sorry, sad and pitiful.

It was hardly walking...

Teetering and falling

Struggling to stand at all...

I woke knowing the cat was someone.

Someone suffering and lonely,

Tired and scared

But who?

Again last night I saw

A cat..

Same cat.

Longing look in his eyes

Now starving ...with a

Belly full of bugs.

Who dear God is this cat?

Who is this person trying so hard to stand?

Pushing forward without strength

Or support, family or friends?

Let me know father and I will go.

I was hushed by the vision

And laid my head down.

Jesus spoke to me...

Doctors come for the sick

Not the well.

To seek the lost

Not the found.

I got up from my bed

I went to the bathroom and stared at myself in the mirror.

There I saw...

I
Saw a cat.

Satan the Power Ranger

He made no boasts of being a Christian. In fact he asked me not to prove just how much he hated God. The whole Jesus thing made him want to puke. "I mean really" he went on to say, "I get the whole blood thing, you know?" "But this guy who drums up some hyper sensitive crowd, gets em to confessin' sins and weeping, then they go to clinging to some myth about this guys blood's gonna heal them..and save them?" "I would never think that way in a million years that Jesus is God's Son and He washes sins away." "Go on tell me another fish tale!" " That joke is old, I don't serve some super hero power ranger named Jesus!"

"I serve the real power of this world...satan."

I just smiled and gave him my twenty dollar bill and paid for my ear to be pierced. I wanted a hole in only one ear. So he marked the spot, opened sterile tools, got the needle,

clamped it through and I started bleeding. Not just a bit, not just a dab, no the blood was a crimson flow running down my neck.

He then tried to get the little hoop through....

He cursed under his breath and says, "I'm gonna pierce you again," And he's trying to get enough tissues to soak up the blood. So the second hoop goes through and he gets the blood stopped. He clamps the hoop tight so it won't wiggle out and without batting an eye, without so much as a spark of realizing what he said...

He said, "The blood is what heals a wound."

"Just let the water and the blood keep you from infection." "You can let the water surround your wound and it will heal you."

"Oh really," I asked

I know for a fact that you are right." and I paused for emphasis

"But there is no way in this world that your little super hero power ranger satan told you that"

O GOD

THERE THAT TEENAGER SAT ON THE BACK OF HIS TRUCK...
hands waving in the air ,
his mouth just a swearin' and every other word was O GOD this and O GOD that.
Then he hopped off the tailgate and as he grabbed another beer for the road
his friends, too young to worry over the terrible mortality of the combination muttered in unison "O GOD there he goes "
And with taillights flashing he was gone. That blue Z-71 didn't make aroound the corner good and a truck came flying-hit the kid ..
.Parents called---hospital rooms-- surgery---white lights nurses everywhere nurses.
O GOD you could hear that mother cry O GOD
and because of that cry to the Almighty the kid lived.
Confined to a wheelchair for the rest of his life He spent day after day in the dark.
No more soties or tailgates of friends coming around for another round of beer ----just this chair ...O GOD
It was along around the middle of December when he had the dream...
Dreamt the entire wreck, the fire
the metal sheeering off
doors and glass slamming
and there was this figure . A man is his dream in whild white robes , hair tossing around in the wind
his hands reaching and shoving covering and pushing.
This man saved him. He drug him to safety and saved him..
He drug him out of the wreckage into a clearing.
He knelt there in pools of gasoline and blood and with His hand on this kid's head He saved him.
O GOD!
So then this kid asked for a book . All they had was a Bible and gradually the young man came around
read the whole thing ---a couple of times
then he and his chair went off to Bible College...O GOD

THERE HE SAT . still in his wheelchair. A little Southern Country church had taken a chance on this young preacher.

This preacher stuck in a chair.
But when he opened his mouth and spoke of our Lord.. all the people
could say was O GOD .
This wheelchair preacher made God so real
believable even
and the stories were wild ones
and his arms would wave around and his hands would fly
mouth just a singing and every other word was O GOD
Because you see He who has been forgiven much loves much.
So the kid knew his life his dream his destiny was to save others .
To pull them from the wreckage of sin
And from that chair Jesus spoke.
Spoke and wept sang and prayed.
That kid ended up bringing every single friend to the Lord.
And because of GOD
because of our fearless immortal Hero
we can lift each other up
O GOD

I Saw Myself

I teach first grade.
Been a few years now since I have been in the classroom with
Such little ones.
Needing this
Needing that.
Constantly talking out of turn and
Getting up
And getting into
Everyone's business
And saying things like
"She looked at me"
And "He broke in line"
And I declare by the end of the day I want to scream and
Would end up as bald as a cucumber
If it weren't for my love for them.
For the potential I see in them.
And yes they are cute.
After all I had a young son once .
I know they will grow.

And I sit here and see myself .
My heavenly father says..
All you do is ask for this
And beg me for that
You are constantly talking out of turn
Getting up
And getting into
Everyone's business
I know He hears me say things like
Why do the evil people prosper?
And
Why do those who challenge God escape?
And by the end of it all I wonder
Does He wring His hands and shake His royal head?
I am sure if it weren't for His great love for me
For the potential He knows I have
Well He would probably

Give up.
But then I think of this...
He had a young son once too.
He grew and grew and grew and
Then died for my
Ability to just enter in
So when I think of how my problems with these little ones
Multiply like rabbits by the end of the day?
All I do now is look in
A mirror
And see
Myself.

| Surgery

We went in today to
See
The doctor and talk about my
I
The one that has cloudy vision
I see out of all the
Time.
I was strapped to dare not wiggle
As the doctor performed his
Task
And when I realized I could not
Move at all
And that was all
He asked…
My I was in his hands
Yes that self I centered
Will
And he kept the beam shining
And while I held real
Still
He burned the vision clear with his burning yet gentle
Touch
And if I had known it would have been this way
My …I would have cooperated
Much
Much more quickly than an Indian's
Foot
And more precise than a free throw
My I did not challenge him
For I desired to
Look
Above me and
Below
And now I see so
Clearly
And the dross is burned out
Too

For the doctor took it away so
Nearly
And gave me eyes that don't see I but you.
So when you sit and
Ponder
And worry over
Sin
Just remember there is an
I
In the center of that word so yes try
Again.
For when we take the "I" out and put an "O"
In there
We see the
Son
Instead of
Sin
And that is the lord's
Affair!!!!!!!!!!

I Wish We Had All Been Ready

Today the news said
"Hurry!" "Hurry!"
"Get here fast !"
"For this sale just won't last!"
And we snapped our fingers
In dismay
To have not been ready
For the big sale day.

Graduation day finally came
Everyone filed down the row
In a practice exercise
Display of achievements
Among the wise
My friends were wondering where I was
I wasn't ready to walk because..
I did not go.

My date had called and asked me out
I ran around the house and shouted
Screaming and dancing out his name
But when he showed at my door
I never came. I was not ready don't you see
For him to go out with a girl like me.

The team went out onto the floor
Dribbling basketballs feeling sure
And for the crowds they all displayed
Their best talents of baskets made.
But when the announcer shouted my name
I just was not ready so I never came.

Achievements, awards,and dates too
Don't always come that easy to you
And when it is these things so easy
It can prepare us for a few less breezy
Trials in life that come our way

Because there are some things more
Important than play.

Take for example the second coming of Christ
And how it would be if we didn't show up that night?
He would leave us here left behind
Because we just never found the time
To get ourselves ready for sales
We would not walk down graduate aisles
Dates, or games were out for me
And I had never practiced being ready you see
So now I sit here left behind and dead
Because you see I was not ready.

If a Picture Paints a Thousand Words

If a picture paints a thousand words
Then why aren't there more....
Museums?
Why aren't there more....
Famous artists?
Namely women artists?
We are the ones yacking and the
Ones appreciating art.

And if a picture is that great that it can take the place of
conversation...
Well why aren't we hanging around office depot to cash in on the
paper sales?

What happened to your mouth now huh?
Oh you don't know what to say?
Why?
Okay I have it....
You were just handed canvas and
A brush.

If People Were God

If we were God
Oh my
Oh my
We would choose only our
Friends to skip through
And get
By.
And they would just
Soar
And
Fly...
Through
Anything they wanted
To
Try.
And what would we do if we were
God?
We would find a way
To
Clap and loudly
Applaud

Now if on the other hand they were not our
Friends
Well that would be where our tolerance
Ends.
And especially if they suffered with something that we
Didn't...
This would be our response toward
Them...
We would justify our hot mouth
And send them
To the curb, deep deep
Down
South
Yes down they
Would

Go
Because to us they'd deserve it ya
Know
And on their way down there
We would send them with tongue lashing
And swear!
After all its only
Fair!
And it serves them right we do
Declare!
For we all do the same things
Every day
As if for our own sins
We have
Paid
And we forget
Christ came
Anyway.
But we choose to judge each sin according to
Us
And when we do that it leads to
Arrogance
For when so perfect we
Are?
And can stand with the father in the heavens
Far...
And help him decide who gets the hot and who goes free
It just may be
Surprising....
The ones we sent away wishing them
well
Knew the father
And we couldn't
Tell
For it is not by our selves that saves our
Souls
It's not up to us
So that no man can
Boast

But it is a gift from God
Alone
For none of us can ever say
That
We
Can accept or reject
Accordingly
We should pray for mercy from it
All
Because the truth is we are not
God.

If You're Not Smart Enough

If you're not
Smart enough
To come in
Out of the rain...
Then can't you
Buy a raincoat?

If you're not
Smart enough
To fight your
Way out of a
Wet paper bag...
Can't you have it
Bagged in plastic
The next time?

If you can't kill
Two birds with
One stone...
Then at least
Put them in a cage
And let them
Keep you company
For a while.

And if you can't
Stand to be at
The end of your rope?
Well next time
Don't just go
Climbing all over
The face of that cliff.

If you feel the
ice underneath
And you're lacing
Up a pair of skates?

Just wait about
A minute and
The ol' sun will
Come out strong
And you can leave
Your shoes on.

If it is too hard
To have two birds
In the hand with
One in the bush?
Stick with hedges

If the nervousness
Is like cats on hot
Tin rooftops?
Remember dogs walk
On solid ground.

And finding
A penny heads
Up brings bad
Luck instead of good?
Hang on your dollars
Forget the pennies.

Keep your friends
Close but your
Enemies closer?

Would you jump off a cliff if your friends did?

Would you deny
Yourself
And take up a
Cross and follow
a man you never met?
Probably not.

Would you lay
Down your life
To find it
Deny yourself
The world to
Inherit it ?
Na ...
And put treasure
In an unseen heaven ?
Nope.
Then just stay
On out there in
The rain...and use
The paper bags
For sackin'
Forget the cage
you don't have
Your birds,
And the skates?
Just keep lacing .
Put your pennies
In a jar with
A tight lid
Because your
Enemy
Just ran off
With the harness
You were gonna
Use for the cliff
You jumped ....

See to it that no one calls you foolish.

If you're not
Smart enough
To come in out
of the rain....
Then you won't
follow someone

You have never met
... down a path you
Don't know ...
Put your treasure
In a place you
have only heard about
...and follow a
Calling loaded
with suffering ,
Hardship,
Tumult, and sorrow.
so then how about that rain?

It Doesn't Mean You're Qualified

Yes, you have five children and I know, I know they sit side by side all in a row, dressed in their little dresses and matching socks. They even have matching hair bows...I'm glad for you really I am. And I know they never do anything wrong. You have never had one minutes trouble out of any of them.

But that doesn't make you qualified to tell me about my one son who rolls his eyes cusses, spits tobacco, drinks some, lives for no ones rules but his own, and would not dead with matching anything in church..... but every child is different and just because you five are perfect doesn't make you qualified to tell me about my one.

Yes I know you have saved every penny. You hold onto a dollar like Ko-Ko the ape holds onto crayons. In fact you are so stuck to your money it reminds me of the time I got gum stuck in my hair . It was stuck there for hours. You know how I spend the stuff but there are reasons for that and just because you are great with money doesn't give you the right to say how I should spend mine.

As for your Christian walk?

Yes, I know you have 30 minutes of quiet Bible study time twice a day. You teach Sunday school sing in the choir and I know you single handed support three missionaries. You give a tenth of your check to the little kid in India and helped build that church and school in Mexico last year. You are such an awesome Christian!!!!

It still doesn't mean you're qualified to tell me.

Gosh, there have been times when I have doubted whether God even existed. I have walked through such dark dark times I sure could have used you singing to me. I have been homeless too and you never built me anything I have been hungry and never saw a dime of your money I've truly had to force myself to pray at all.

When it comes to spending time you aren't ever home you visit the poor the shut-ins the sick and the orphans...but you never came to see me. No your shadow never did darken the doorway. So no, you are not qualified to tell me of the wasted years of drinking and partying. Yes I know you have had the same fantastic job for the last 35 years. So no you are not qualified to know what it is like to not have one for three months and then go from job to job for the next six months....you just would not understand. And your clothes ?well I see you wear all that designer fashion jazz..mine ???Well they come from garage sales

and thrift stores. Eating and exercise? I watch you chase a lettuce leaf
around on your plate and of course work out at the most prominent
gym why didn't you just renew your membership last week?
And as for your friends yes how sweet they are all from your Sunday
school class.
Okay okay... some of mine mess around and drink and
okay a few have served time and have gone through divorces...

Two men went to pray.
One said...
"I give tithe, I support three missionaries
I sing in the choir and I give to the kids in India ...I manage my money,
my time, my friends, and my eating, exercise, and work."

The other man said....
"Lord have mercy on me a sinner I can not manage one thing."
Who among you is qualified?
Qualified to be a judge ?
For in the way you judge that same way
You will be judged.
Qualified or not.

It Is All About Money

It is all about money they shouted at the rally...
Well finally someone said from the back...
Finally someone was honest about this fundraiser crap.
It had been all about money for years and years...
The cure had long been found and the money?
The money was a by product of pride...
Pride and nothing more that was used as a measuring device
To show how very high they had all become..
To demonstrate how very important they had all become
And it marked the finishing positions of their
Family names...and how very remembered they had been.

It is all about money they shared professionally among themselves
Well someone finally said from the boardroom table...
Finally someone was honest about this buy out crap.
It had always been about money and they used it for an "I'm power-
fuller
Than you gig..."
Used for I can get by with underhandedness...
Yes it had become an I can treat people any ol' way I want to type thing
Because the boss had money...and was about to get a bunch more
He could prove his value by it
He proved his family by it
He proved he had been here on earth by it...right?

It is all about money they whispered around the kitchen table.
Well someone said from their place at the stove...
Finally someone was honest about dealing drugs...
It had always been about money
And power and honor among men...
Who had the clothes the women the clubs the weapons
Who was running from whom and who had the power to place fear
terror and
Revenge within the hearts of innocent the opposing gangs the man
down the street
Running the convenience store
It was all about money never would it change..

And it goes on and on and on
With athletes,
With office
With education
With medicine
With possessions of every kind.
And we think we can buy anything...
We think we can ruin everything....
We think we are omnipotent.
Omniscient
And omnipresent...
While all this time
Since the earth was void of shape and color and sound..
The whole thing was set into being with his..
Voice.
The whole earth depends on his
Breath...
Our futures hinge on this man's...
Blood.
And it never once mattered about money.
It cost much much more ...
It costs people their lives....
And when we figure out how to give that up for a fundraiser
Or sacrifice that in a business deal..
Exchange a couple 20 years for choice cut drugs...
The way he did???
We are worthless.

"Lay not up for yourselves treasure on earth where moth and rust can
Destroy where thieves can break in and steal..
But lay up for yourselves treasures in heaven
Where neither rust nor moth can destroy neither thieves break in and
steal...
For where your treasure is there is your
Heart
Also."

It Is Easy

It is too easy to sit and agree
With all of the sins that you see in
Me.
And you shake your head and smile a
Bunch
But you just don't get it you're as guilty as
Much
And the thing of it is you love to
Hear
Me confess sin so loud and
Clear
But you to do it?
No my dear.
And I worry that you are bound with
Ropes
Invisible ones that give you false
Hopes.
And the strength you trust in
Is yours
Alone…
It simply amazes me puts me to
Shame
The ways I admit to the guilt and bad ways
But you cant ever ever take the
Blame.
Why? Its easy!!!!!!!!

It Isn't Enough

It isn't enough to be close to the rain
To feel it from inside your
Window pane

And it isn't enough to be close to the mall
You'd get nothing purchased
Nothing at all..

And as for the fishing?
Just take a look it isn't enough
To just bait a hook.

It isn't enough to say I like you
When love's what you feel
Tender and true

And when you consider your
Summer vacation?
And your travels will take you
To see your relation?

You have to do more than
Just fill up with gas
It isn't enough to just look at a map.

And so I think you see my plight
Lacing up boxing gloves
Doesn't mean that you'll fight

And you may talk and act all brave
But it isn't enough are you really
Saved?

Because you're good of course I say "yes"
But it isn't enough for heaven's rest

Close is good for horseshoes
But not when it comes to your soul
To lose...

And bombs too it is enough
to wipe out countries
Leave them torn up and rough

So if you think your decision is tough?
You cant just think about it
It isn't enough.

It Was a Moose

When I was seventeen I shot a moose, I crawled 300 yards or so through the snow on my belly with the 270 rifle and scope on my back and with the snake river in the background I saw a female moose with her baby. They were foraging as we call it or simply put looking for food. But I trained the scope on her head and when I fired the gun she went down. I could only kill one animal legally and my mother had a permit so she killed the calf.

I had a ring around my eye dripping blood from getting too close to the scope. But it didn't stop me from taking the pistol and shooting the mother in the head to finish her off. I gutted her too with my dad's hunting knife and quartered her with a chain saw. Then with a rope around my waist I hauled the beast out of the woods.

Satan then sat back on his heels and asked "How's that for a days work boys?" "Not bad taking em both out." And the demons hold their sides laughing and thinking about how big moose are and how it was no trouble shooting one in the head.

But the Lord on the other hand looks down upon all creatures. Even moose.

And He sees them in the dead of winter trying hard to find food . They scrape at the snow with their feet and their legs and the bellow out a squeal letting other mothers know where they are...

Sometimes God in his mercy takes em on home.

He sees what they will be up against and with his eyes trained on them He will allow the shooting.

And so that the baby wont be orphaned? He allows the mom too, to be taken up.

In heaven it sounds something like this. We have received a worn weary soul and her child. Shot in the head both of them and gutted.

The underworld claims the victory for the slaying but the souls do not lay in their hands.

They may be responsible but they are not caretakers of these. No, they belong to the Lord. "but" asked one "on earth they will think the God of hosts did this" "They will blame Him and they will turn away from Him"

The righteous Father with blazing eyes and hair of fire turned and said"What does it matter to me the opinion of satan?" "and who

is man to be mindful of me?" "Know ye not that nothing happens without my approval for the children who are 'the called'?"
And the angels are silent.

I shot a moose when I was just seventeen and you know something? It wasn't the first time God raised a big ol moose from the dead …
And her baby too.

Settled for Being Bait

The man sat at his desk...
No one around
It was after 5:00
Even the boss had gone home..
Come to think of it?
He may not have come in today at all.
Earlier that day he caught sight of
A picture sent on his phone...had no time to look at it so
What the heck
No one around....
It was after 5:00
Couldn't hurt
To pull it up
On the computer..
He had one finger on
"delete"
One finger on "download all"
One push
And images so raw
So extreme
So graphic
Busted through
The volume....
My God!
How loud did he have this thing?
The oooosssszzzzyyy and oannningss
And come on babbbyyy you know you
Want it this ways...screamed out of the monitor.
For a moment
Time was suspended and the delete button
Hid from him like a coy little bunny in a garden.
Finally he found his bearings and the whole scene went dead.
He clicked "Shut down and log off"
And then straightened his tie adjusted his coat..
And before he was through?
He looked up.
There peering over the cubicle barrier was

The boss.
Can I see you a minute please he asked
No emotion at all...
Before you're through?
Sure I was just getting ready to leave..uh yea
I can stop by no problem..
And they sat apart from each other by about six feet or so...
Just staring
Just grasping for words like fish do for minnows
As bait..not realizing the minnows are fish too.
Before they're through..
And he said
"Hope it was worth it"
Before you're through take a minute and consider a few things
Your job is gone
Your wife is disappointed
Self respect is both
And daughter is unprotected...
Your reputation is lost
And so is your pride
Your friends shake their heads and
Shuffle your things in a box...
So before you're through take one long look at
The reason...
And there in his hands
He held up a picture of the nude threesome
Graphically shoving unspeakable objects in
Unbelievable places with unreserved unabashed shameless eyes
And they not knowing they were fish too
Had settled for being bait...

And When God Didn't Destroy Nineveh?

Jonah
Was
Furious!
How dare God spare that wicked city?
After all the chances
And all the warnings
And all the sermons?
Man!
And they were living
Parading around full of sin!
Just like the coworker last week that didn't get fired
Boy I watched as you sat back
On your laurel butt
Wishin' he'd get his
Punishment
And when he didn't?
Well it made me think of
The time you deserved to run out of gas
But I didn't allow it .
And how about the time you should have gone without food or shelter
for the ways you were living? Huh?
You didn't because I would let it happen...and how about the storm
that should have wrecked your house and tore your roof off but I didn't
let the weather touch you.
Do you have any idea of how badly you deserved to be slowed down?

So please do not come asking me to condemn someone for sin.
Remember Jonah?
I wonder what would happen if a fish found it's way to your front porch
to swallow you up to
Shut you up
And to slow you down.
Because, that fish tank in your living room?
Don't put it past me.

Jumpers

One day the girl just woke up----
She had been unconscious
For years.

Her husband and her family had waited
Wringing their hands beside her bed and
Persevered in prayer.
Her friends were grieving too
How could this girl –so young –so full of energy and life
have fallen?

She just walked up ten flights of stairs to
The upper balcony and
Jumped.
There wasn't noticeable damage from the
First jump and it did capture people's
Attention…. So
When she climbed the stairs and jumped again
And
Again
And
Again
And
Again?
And three years later she was limping up the flight
Crawling up the last set of stairs to
Jump?
Well her coma
Was no surprise.
And this time her friends hung their heads and
Walked away….

\\\\\\\\\\\\\\\\\\\\\\\\\\\\\\\\\\\\\\\
She was not moving
\\\\\\\\\\\\\\\\\\\\\\\\\\\\\\\\\\\\\\\

Her birth angel ran to Jesus.
"Master come quickly she has fallen..."
Jesus went to the place where the girl lay.....
Scoffers
Mockers
Demons
And even hell itself
Like feasting vultures were closing in.
The girls angel told those faithful few
Who still remained
"He is come"
And He brushed the hair out of her eyes and
The touch of his hand
Caused her eyes to open.
She is not dead ...
Only sleeping..Jesus said
He said unto all those who are
Blind
Wretched
Demon possessed
Angry
Adulterous
Gossipers
Idolaters
Arrogant
Prideful
Thieves
And yes
The
Continuous ....jumpers
Go and sin no more..
I am come
So you
Wont......Jump.

Just As I Am

I'm just this way I heard you say
As you cut me to the core
With your tongue I am undone cant stand it anymore

And I just cant change so don't assume that I will ever <u>try</u>
for I am glued and so far gone that you'd never ever <u>pry</u>...

Off the grit sand off the grime and shred the thick hard crust why I
have years of hate its not a crime to bury bitterness disgust

Its who I am so deal with it you keep on saying to me and when I cant
and want to quit you continue on your spree

Of cursing and of hurtful spray and the pain you cause wont land you
justify and then deny saying its just the way I am.

God knows the truth he can not accept the ways you are so cruel He
shed His blood yes He's wept and He begging you to do it too.

For His only son did not wait for all of us to be the kind of people full
of grace and mercy too he'd be proud to not leave behind.

The excuse of what you say that this is who you are? God wont think
you are right and you wont get very far.

Remember oh please remember that His original plan was to save each
type of sinner for me just as I am.

Just as I am without one plea but that thy blood was shed for me and
that thou bidst me come to Thee oh Lamb of God I come ...I come.

Just Ask David

When David was younger---
Just a new king
He could not focus
Think about war or
Anything.
He was all busy trying to
Feel big
And ended up with issues that
He'd purposefully rigged...
So early hours one day he arose.

And went out on his balcony the only
He froze.
For what did his wandering eyes should see
But Bathsheeba lovely thing bathing.

Who is that beauty why she looks like a queen
I want her as mine more than
Anything.
And what was to follow
What s what
And
That's that---
Just about took David down to the mat.
And all through the bible men struggle
You see with eyes and surprise infidelity.
So why do you think Jesus warned men
About prolonged stares and the lustful mention
He saw the girls with tops far too low and pants way too tight but what
he wants to know is how focused you'd stay on the wife of your youth
and how honest your heart is yes tell the truth
For your wife sees the fruit on your ol' vine
She sees your eyes travel she is not blind---
And in James too it says lust of eyes drags us away
It is common among folks so don't shake your head
If you can honestly keep a boundary up when a scantily clad waitress
comes

To fill your cup—
If your heart knows no twinge no jolt or lost focus the you have a
handle on things I'd say you're not bogus but if you are all over the
board say stuff thinking and maybe imagining more....
Then all you really need to do is take an example from a book or two
And see how all that affected their loved
Because as far as I know it created pain and strife and if you were
willing and if we were able
All wed have to do is just go ask David.

Just Enough

The man stood there
Warming his hands at the campfire
He and his buddies had built.
A roaring beauty
The thing shot off blue and yellow sparks
Deep into the night.
They took turns telling stories of other
Camping trips
Other fires.
And then there was a silence.
Dug down deep and even brought tears to
Their eyes as
One of the men told the story of how three years
Back, Shawn got too close to the fire.
Just not payin' attention..
Just playing
Just thought he's see how close he could get to the
Flame.
What he didn't know was as he
Took the one step closer and then the other
Chuck had slipped off to grab another beer.
Coming back half tipped he slapped
Shawn on the back.."hey Shawn think you can
Get any closer?"
Shawn lost his balance and toppled
Stumbled into the flames.
He didn't mean too
And Chuck has carried the guilt to this day.
Hasn't been on a guys night out since.

There are certain things in life
The devil is begging us to do.
And it does not have to be all the way.
It can just be "close enough"
Because all he has to do then
Is give a little push.
He knows.
He's livin' pretty close to a fire himself.

I Went Weak in the Knees

I went weak in the heart to see that child gaze into my eyes and honestly say "I want to be just like you "

I couldn't believe my ears..like me? Me?

who would wish that on themselves? Oh who?

for with that wish comes a great great price.

A cost tremendously high a sell out ---that's how high...a sell out.

and looking back into time --time before selling out ...I see myself.

I was nothing like the normal. Nothing predictable or the same. I knew early on the deepness of a soul. I knew.

I saw the shallowness of the other stuff which is everything else.

and I felt your nudge. Holy pushing out of the nest and I fell out.

but it didn't take long to see that living a holy life was hard.

yes it was as hard to do as the ground I fell on.

and it was just like you to come.

as wind you twirled me into a direction.

as rolling thunder challenged me too.

as a light light feather you soothed my grounded body.

but I just wasn't like you.

I was a tornado taking in as much --living out loud as much --and destroying as much as I could.

I was thunder too --I was .

But then you came again as light

With the flickering rays of a simple candle you calmed my booming heart.

that's just like you.

quick as a twitch from a harness that binds --I shrugged you off.

I wandered away far far far away.

It happened one day and it's just like you to send someone after me calling my name.

and not to send me further away--it was just like you to have it be

a child.

so as I let myself ease back from that moment of remembering,

And I look down to see the child intently waiting for an answer..

all I can say is

"Darling I had to become just like you."

Just Looking

I was profoundly distressed at myself today.
I had written a piece …a story about people with hardship.
And although I know hard times and toil is relative…I was aghast at
my own arrogance.

Because what do I know about just looking?

I cant do it anywhere I go .

I can't just look at Wal-Mart.
Or at any fine jewelry counter, and I cant just look when it comes to
say…
Others fashion sense or
How about cars?
Houses?
Or activities?
No
I have to be the center of it all.
And I was actually blushing
Over it
I was.

You see today
Today I realized that
That was exactly all she'd ever
Been able
To do
Is look.
At others walk
And play
Sing
And run or even plan to
Skip
Or shop or paint or
God knows not to even dare to climb.

And I in my profound distress
Was so angry at those who become frustrated with their
Slowness
And their shyness
Or how about the ramps that cities build?
Frustration over reserved parking spots?
Or how about special money for them every month?
Angry?
Well
You shouldn't be
Because you see
All you're doing is
Looking.

And as long as we all miss it by
So vast
A measure?

The physically challenged will run away with
The prize every single time

And leave the rest of us
Just looking.

Just Two Little Kids

Two little boys were playing
In their backyard
One pushed a red truck
And the other a car

And the play time was usual
It really was
Until a horsefly over their heads
Came to buzz

The boy with the truck
Bore down a look of fright
The other child noticed the
Terror in his eyes

And to watch what the two
Of them did just then
Told me a lot of how they'd
Turn out to be men

For the one who motored
The truck
You know the first one who
Was frightened and such?
Did the natural thing
People <u>do</u>
He screamed and he
Hollered and waved his arms
Through
The air.

The second little boy all
Blonde, blue eyed fair
Told his friend to stop
Waving his arms in the air

Said "Come real close I'll tell
You what"
"We'll let that bugger land and then
We will swat
Him real hard"

It took a moment to reach that
Agreement between
Because of course the questions
That were obviously seen

Was which boy was willing
To let land
A mighty, fierce horsefly
On his arm or hand?

The boy with the truck
Shook his head no
There was no way he'd
Offer arm or hand to hold
A fly

So the other child who
Pushed the car
Told his buddy he'd do it
So "Stay where you are"

They heard the low humming
The drone of the fly
And then it hovering and
Those two blue-black big eyes

Just as was planned it landed
Upon the kid
And he sat there frozen
The weight upon his
Face

To kill the fly was the
Purpose, the goal
But would he slap himself
Or would his friend
Be that bold?

And to my surprise the two
Kids that day
Two innocent children who had
Gone out to play

Held still as stars
Suspended in space
And the truck moving boy
Struck the blonde in the face

The blow wasn't light
It was unusually severe
To strike a friend that hard
In the face above the ear
That way.

The kid who was hit
Sat real tight
And the boy simply asked
"Is he dead all right?"

"Yep got him"
Came the reply
But with the results
Also evolved a black eye
For the boy.

And seeming to not notice
Or ponder or care
The toe-headed boy
The one who was fair?

Reared back his fist
Packed in and tight
And struck the other kid
With all his might.
In the face.

"Was there a bug
On my face too?"
"For that was something
You shouldn't do!"

"No" whispered the first
Kid that day
But you deserved it for hitting
My face.

"But that was our plan it was
The rule"
"But you did not have to hit
Me that cruel"

"Well" said the second
You are already struck
And went back to moving
The little red truck

And likewise the child
With bruised ear and eye
Holding the now dead
Monstrous horsefly

Looked square at his friend
Who he'd punched in the face
And said and you know how it feels to be in my place
Without a bug.

They dropped their toys
They did not smile
They stopped playing
Cars and trucks for a while

And the one kid turned
To the other and said
Do you remember what
Our Sunday school teacher read?

No what said the other
While he looked away
What did she read ?
Well what did she say?

She read that there was
A big bad old devil
Who came up around us
Yep, came up from hell

And tried to kill a king
just a …. fly baby
With shepherds and sheep
And even cows maybe
Looking on

And without it deserved
The people crushed the 'baby' fly
And slapped him and even caused
Him to die.

But I thought said the other
Boy fast
That he wasn't the kind to
Hit people back!

Well said the blonde with
A crooked smile
That was him and I am me
And He's been gone for awhile..

But I think I also heard our
Sunday teacher say
He'll return again for undeserved
Punching to pay.

And that was when the
Kid realized it
That he should not have
Balled up his fist.

Knitting

Knittin' needles just a flyin'
She could watch TV
And knit
She could sit at a ballgame
And knit
She could go to church on a Sunday night
And knit
Potholders
Sweaters
Scarves
Anything she put those needles to turned out perfectly.
I saw her out the other day
Pickin' out yarn
She was choosin' real careful like and getting enough for the project
So's she wouldn't leave the blanket or sweater or scarf undone
Cause you know the store may just up and discontinue that shade
or somethin' irregular like that.
So's I say "Hello" and let her get back to her knittin'.
And you know God is like that.
He has those knittin' needles
Just a flyin'
And they are trained on forming that human.
He doesn't knit sweaters and such
But sacred soul filled
Personality blessed
Children
His purpose is to knit together
Children with promise
Lives full of purpose.
And yet
We wonder why disease takes our youngins'
Or untimely death
Or sometimes unexplainable
"no" answer times too
And we wonder

"Did God run out of yarn"?
Or maybe he couldn't concentrate on that old war and knit at the
same time..
And we lift our tear filled eyes to him and breathlessly ask "Why?"
Gently He puts down his knittin' and
Explains that there are things we don't know about that lie
in waitin' for that baby or child.
He spares them either future suffering
Or continued
And we
Wish
For
More
Of
It
For
Them?
We do?
God is not watchin' ballgames or out sittin' on a river bank fishin'
With a knittin' bag boilin' out a rainbow of colored yarn and such.
He knows when those youngins' need to stop
And come on in
Don't worry they are sittin' at the table with the king.

You know the other day
I saw God
Pickin' out yarn
He was
All colors
I imagined him using that real
Pretty blue for a little boy's eyes
And the tan for arms
And legs
I stopped to say "Hello"
He turned and hugged my neck.
I was gonna take that minute to ask him about some of those
unfinished knittins' I'd seen lately.
But you know? He was there choosin' colors and concentratin'

So I know He's thinking of someone special for your family
And those that leave?
Well they are finished works of promise bringin' glory to the king
So now you just don't worry bout' that and let him get back to
Knittin'.

Mighty Warrior

This is a part of God I forgot about
He will and does descend with a Holy shout
He takes back possession of those who are truly His
He wont hand these over if they are His kids
He fights the battles for us while we but merely stand
Held captive by his arms and in His almighty hands.
Sometimes we get all taken in the thought that God is love
And the truth is that it is so
But He fights for us through blood.
He is the warrior the commander the Lord of hosts is He
And the path that the opponent considers stays Him at his feet.
He is the only winner the only ruler too
And when the fall's turned to winter He still fights for me and you
So don't get all fluffy in thinking all is soft
Because there wasn't anything easy about the bloody cross
And so we see love defined yes we see love built more
In this that God fights for us and He is our warrior!

My Jesus I Love Thee

My Jesus I love thee
When things are just fine
When the rain and the bills
Stay clear from my skies

I love thee for wearing
The thorns on thy brow
But only when I suffer
So don't bother me now

For yes I know thou art mine
And now's as good a time as any
For I am happy and fulfilled
I know I have more than plenty

There's no other savior
I'll hold to but thee
And as long as I get
What I want, what I see

You can just stay a picture
In some book or magazine
And for me it's no matter
You're not real just a painting

Wait oh no what? What is it dear?
Our child was killed the other
Is not doing real good
Yes it is his brother?

And what's more you said?
You meant the family down town
Who had the wife that you say
Has been running around?

My wife? What did you say?
She is not the type and she
Loves adores and is faithful
Why she is loyal to me!

So now I have two sons who
Have died they are dead
And the wife of thirty years
Forsaken our vows when we wed.
Could I have one more chance to
Sing that song another verse
And I promise I will be serious
I will practice ..rehearse!

My Jesus you are not a bright picture
And you are the only one
Who can fix my life my marriage
For you are Christ the son

You have suddenly become so
Much more to me now
I have lost everything and
I humbly surrender and bow.

I believe you to be the only way
And realize the context of
What you have done for me
When you rose and ascended above.

I sit on my couch here all silent
And I sit here in this room alone
But I watch you get up from the
Grave and God rolled the stone.

Why did I have to lose everything?
Just to believe you and see
You are Jesus the son of God
And I have nothing, nothing but Thee.

My Will

My will was read in a dream I had had
The other night while I lay in my bed
And to my surprise this is what was said:

To my son dearest son
My only one true
I
Bequeath my sour temper to
You…
And for your inheritance all I
Possess of my past revenge and
Loneliness.

I give you now my hate filled heart
Over unfulfilled promises and dreams
I could not start
And

For the rest of your life digging a well
I bequeath to you a race from disaster's swell.

Well out of that dream I awoke in a sweat
Scared panic stricken
And the linens soaked …wet

And crawled out of bed got down
On my knees
And begged my savior for
Another dream please?

So this is what the father
Did do
He put me to sleep
And before the nights through
He came to me
Softly and said

Please fulfill this
My dear daughter in your head

Leave the revenge up to me for to
You I leave peace of mind
And strength I
Bequeath

And dear one rest confident
My eyes have not shut against the
Arrogant..
I will never leave you or forsake
You it's true
So sleep on in safety
I'll prosper you..
I'll broaden your territory
And strengthen your run
And before it is over you'll see a redeemed son
Stay focused stay ready and steadfast until
The time comes for opening the book to my will

Near to the Heart of God

She wept gut wrenching sobs over the stillborn child. Just sat on the edge of that cold hospital bed and with her head in her hands she sobbed.
Thump,thump
Thump, thump
Do you hear that? The angels were there. She was drawn in and held tight...yes she stopped her crying and listened. She was near to the heart of God.

Losing that race was significant. His girlfriend was there his mom and dad but his little brother was there too probably thought "gosh he wasn't all that great"
"Can't even win anything!"
The disappointment was humiliating. As he raised the gun to his temple he heard something.
Thump,thump
Thump,thump
What was that?
Had he pulled the trigger?
Count fingers pull some hair. Am I alive?
Angels had drawn him into the great arms of God.

"You would have loved my dad" he would always say
He stayed by us through the dark days of the depression. He would sneak upstairs late at night I know because I would hear them creaking with his weight. One night I followed him up and from behind a pile of quilts I saw my father praying. All wrapped up tight. Folded in like he was wrapped up into the heart of God.
And baby, that is where I have placed you.
With our laughing mouth and beautiful eyes. I have laid you in the arms of God. Listen. Do you hear that?
Thump, thump
Thump, thump
Yes darling you are near to the heart of God.
You are that close.

New Balance

I saw the new balance shoes lying on the step
I know when we wear them they give a lot of pep.
But what does a person do if the shoe just won't go?
Do we vow to give up and in the trash do throw?
Or do we say to our selves "I'll get buy"
And continue my dreams ..reach for the sky?
My life isn't dictated by this curtain's valance.
And a shoe really can't offer a person new balance.

That my friend comes strictly from the father.
So in you own strength? Why, don't even bother.
You will only disappointment find
And confusion, depression and anguish of the deepest kind.
It may be possible to appear put together.
And to the outside world you'll pretend to face the weather.
So don't trust, depend upon or accept another challenge.
Only in the Christ, the host of heaven offers new balance!

No Not One

From the beginning God was not into
Showing off
He could have come as
King Kong or as a monster or some great military hero like Napoleon
but to come as a Baby?
And I notice that that is exactly how each of us come into the
World.

And he announced his birth to the lowest the dirtiest , the coarsest of
all society the poorest of all...
Shepherds

And when they stood around that manger and their
Long dirty hair swept off their faces into His?
Of all the professions to become.. That is what He became...
A shepherd
Then it was time to start preachin'
He called the coarsest, toughest filthiest 12 men
Strong from slinging nets and catchin' fish
Follow Him.

Hauling up the lost
Napoleon or King Kong could have done it.
But of all the miracles...
He became a fisherman.
He got filthy and tough and he ended up pushin' sweaty hair out of His
face .
He rolled up His sleeves and cast nets too
And He's still waitin' for them to completely fill.
But He if hadn't the greatness to become one of us He would never
save one of us.
No not one.

No One Came

This morning on the
News
A
Woman in an emergency room
Was caught on tape
Squirming and fidgeting
In her chair.
She ended up
Piled up
And sprawled out on the floor
A couple of guards came in
To where she was and
While she was lying there they shrugged
And went back to work..
A doctor came in and checked on her and turned
And left

A nurse finally kicked her in the leg
To see if she would respond
When she did not move they
Pronounced her dead
And hauled the body off.
That reality shakes me
Down something awful
Kind of
Deep
It was all caught on camera
And
No one
Came.

On the morning news there was a
Woman who was in an emergency room waiting to be seen.
She was caught on camera squirming and fidgeting
But when she
Ended up in the floor
The guards came

And went
And the doctor
Came
And went
And she laid there
When she had the strength
She opened her eyes and saw angels hovering close
She tried to move and
It just took so much energy
And with that pain in her
Head
Well
She knew angels didn't show up for just no good
Reason.
Hot tears ran
Just like the help.
She never thought she would end up like this and you know?
Sometimes
Our Father
Gets enough
He saw her there in the floor.
And He sent the angels....
She was happy to crawl into
Their arms
And she felt the floor lift away as they flew
She was free and satisfied yes
Happy to go
When no one came.

Oh Little Town of Bethlehem

Every year anyone who's anyone in the Muslim world makes a trip to
Mecca, the birthplace of Mohammed. And year After year After year
They make the journey to see a
dead king
If men could look upon the bones
The sacred bones of Mohammed?
Don't you think they'd get it?
He's still there!
They are vowing
And bowing to a dead king.
Now think of this.
Bethlehem was visited once
By a baby.
And if we the saints of God
Kept up a yearly march to see Him?
To worship at His tomb?
Remember
He's not there.
He's gone.
His bones no longer lay around.
So both trips would be a wasted journey...
One to visit powerless bones,
the other to visit a powerless grave.
The little town of Bethlehem was visited once by the King of Kings
that's all it needed
And the people still didn't get it.

On the Water

Depressed
Given
Up
Just go back to what you know....
Jesus was crucified and
Dead almost three days
But
Of all those to see him it was
Peter.
Peter saw the lord
And the Christ said
"Come"
Walk with me upon the water...
Tread upon the waves
And conquer the roar of the wind
Turn a deaf ear to the opinions
Ignore all other sounds...
In a second peter scrambled over the side of that
Rugged fishing boat
He walked to the master....
Yes
Peter walked on the water.

And you know ???
Maybe he needed to have something carry him
Something huge like that
Something required of him
He had to do something bigger for the Christ than the thing he had
done
Against him
And isn't it like the
Son
Of
God
To
Know
That?

Maybe that is why your ministry is such a success.
Maybe it has to be to convince
You
To challenge you'
To prove to you that
That sin you once lived in against Him is forgiven and
Gone and
Now?
Well now you are
Being asked
To come
To
Step out of that
Rugged old boat you're
In
And walk with Him
On
The
Water.

On the Wrong Track

A pup was crossing a busy highway
Probably just finished at his friends house that day
And on his trek home where he stayed
He about got hit and this is
How it happened how it unfolded they say...

Yep just this morning at around nine or ten
My master was feeding me from the kitchen
And it was a beautiful day so I thought I would go
Over to the next door neighbor's or so..
And before I knew why it was noon
And I had been gone a long time it was true..
But rover had been talking about
His last night's partying and roaming around
So I lost all track of time because of that
So I thought "take the shortcut across carver's flats"
And as I popped out of the foliage just so
I saw that I was dumped out on open road.
I looked both ways I mean it I did
But failed to see that car about got hit!
And when the people swerved to miss me
I ran to the other side panicking
And all the rest of the jog to my house
With all of rover's stories rolling around
how he had nearly escaped this and that
I had almost got his share and mine too for a fact
But as I swung into my own driveway
And saw my full food bowl and my water tray
I sat like a good dog and decided right then
That the wanderers life was not for me my friend
It may be the perfect life for dear rover
And sniffing other fields of fresh green clover
Are just as much fun as sitting in sin
But I'll tell you all my playing around? Ended.
For I was just **listening** to other affairs
And how other dogs chose lives that were theirs
And all I was doing was just **heading for home**

And I about met my maker never more to roam.
So this is the moral of this little story..
You can be looking on quite innocently
And still get hit hard from the back
And never realize at all you were on the wrong track.

Once When I Was Young

Once when I was young
I'd think a banana was a gun
And I'd hold it out
"Put your hands up" I'd shout
You could trick me easily
By things that imitatingly
Looked just like the other
Sometimes going under cover
I'd never even guess
The real one would be best
I'd settle for imitations
Of the Lord's creations
And accept the bananas
And biting shapes in sandwiches
To replace a gun in hand
For bananas and sandwiches cant
Protect anyone for real
So don't let the enemy kill
Your knowledge of the truth
If you think he is stupid
He'll make you think a fake
Will defeat him while he makes
You think from a banana comes
Weapons once when I was young.

Only One Way

I sat there waiting in the chair
In the office
In the school I had wanted to teach at for over a year.
The principal was interviewing and I had been called.
Nervous? Not even close! I was so scared I should have worn
something warm because I was shivering .
When the woman ahead of me walked out of his office smart skirt
leather briefcase and perfect black shoes. I mentally looked down at
myself.
Old navy skirt, it was linen but wrinkled, flats instead of heels and a
handbag that looked as though it would belong to bag lady instead of
a prospective teacher. Without warning the principal's voice snapped
me away from my day dreaming and I followed him in.
Once inside I tried to gracefully sit. My foot hung up on the scroll
pattern on the foot of the chair and I almost tripped. It was a good
thing I had on flats! And my skirt went way past my knees when I sat
so I felt that was an example of professionalism. I placed my handbag
in the floor and fumbled around for my resume. Finally I found my
manilla folder and handed him its contents.
He opened the folder. He smiled he laughed he frowned and then he
handed it back to me.
I am sure you are a good person he said.
And you have dressed nicely and behaved appropriately. As for the
resume to be accepted for this position? I just cant hire you. There
is one form only one acceptable form we take here and it is easily
downloaded. You don't have any other options. And I cant let you in
this school without you following the details of the paper.

And you something?
If you sit and think about it ...that is exactly the same hard cold truth
about God and getting into heaven.
We can have the clothes, old or new and the walk and the talk and the
fancy briefcases and such but unless we follow the son of God to the
cross and until we are covered by his blood we aren't going anywhere.
We were never asked to carry a handbag ...rather a cross
Not to walk in heels..rather walk up a hill.

Clothed not in tweed skirts...but rather in Christ
And not approaching him in any ol' form we dream up but rather just one
There is just one way.

Our Pets

All of us have pets.
We take them
Everywhere we go.
And most of the time
If pets aren't allowed
In a mall, or store full of food restaurants
Motels or church?
Well there they are
waitin for us
In the car
With the window cracked
Just enough
To let them breathe.
Sometimes we sneak them in
If they're small
And we hide them
In oversized handbags
or stroll them along
In carriages

We feed them
Play with them
Wc let them eat after us .
they lick our spoons
And faces and sometimes
our feet.

Our pets are great company
They are cute
And funny
And when housebroken
They come inside...
They eat with us ,
Sleep with us
And run around acting
Lively and cute
We walk our pets on leashes.

We love our pets
We protect our pets
When one of them dies
It is like a member
Of the family

And if we could imagine this entire description of pets and how it
could apply to sin?
We would see it all so differently

Would you for instance walk your pet sin of
Porn
On a leash
And walk it around your community?
How about feeding the sin
Of a critical spirit
Ice-cream and fault finding
And crawling
In bed snuggled
Up tight with
Spousal abuse
Or having
The two pups
Of emotional abuse
and verbal abuse
Sleep on your pillow ?
Could you leave the window
cracked
And keep prescription drug addiction
And the pet sin
of the lingering affair
alive in the car
While you are
In church singing in the choir?
Maybe you sneak
he pet sin of
Foul jokes
And foul thoughts

And coarse jokes
In hidden in your
Handbag.

But just let someone
hit that pet sin
And kill it
Maybe with God's word
or just down right good character and we act crushed!
don't ask me to say goodbye to that!
It never hurt
anyone and it
was such good company
So fun and so cute!

Well, if it was
Such great
Company
You may want
to stay with it in the car
with the window cracked....because the pet sin
You tried to hide
Just tore up the leather seats pooped in the floorboard
and slobbered all over the windows....
So now?
Still able to hide that sin
That pet sin?

Passing It Up Or By

Moses when he was such a young baby
Was victim to fear by <u>everyone</u> maybe
But when in the basket he was placed
And sent bobbing along
Without a trace
she scooped him up that day
Never outta'
But of course it was the Pharaoh's daughter
And just like a child who brings home a pup?
This beautiful princess
Couldn't pass it up.
And looking around for a woman to care
Found the boy's mother
Standing there
So the chance once again to fill up her cup?
Would not be... couldn't be ever be passed up.
But Moses grew big and strong in the kingdom nearby
And one day when a worker was running his fly
Moses killed him he just had to die...
It was something he'd think about later
But for right now he was the terminator.
someone saw him and reported him in
Said they had caught him with intentional sin
And so Moses ran to the desert for peace
Until from the curse he was finally released.
Then after 40 years it was time
To get back out there and
Stand up to
Fight.
To set his people free from a master
To give them purpose away from disaster.
And as he stood in front of a bush that burned
The lord God asked "have you, Moses yet completely
Learned?
Moses replied in a begging sort of cry
Send someone else I cant go no, not I
I wont do this thing I will pass it by

I'm a wanted man running away from the sword
But God said "Now you're avoiding the Lord.
This is a chance to show them a God
Who performs mighty wonders
They will scratch heads and nod..
Now in your hand this stick is a rod
But when Moses tossed the stick like a stake
It turned into a slithering coiled up snake
And after that you'd think he'd obey
But that's when the whole conversation began
About how to send another Man
And how he couldn't do this and couldn't do that...
Why the Lord's temper burned down right flat.
And so finally after discussion of such
He let Moses pass it up
And gave him Aaron to help him out
When Moses was stumped Aaron would
Shout
And the two of them went with a battle cry
For they weren't going to
Pass this by.
And as the story
Unfolds
We all read about the curses....
Oh those?
Yes and finally the death angel shows his mighty punch
But with the blood of the lamb?
He'd pass you up.
So Christian oh Christian when you think life's
Over
And you cant take , juggle or handle any
More
Just remember if you are covered by the lambs
Blood from on
High
These wicked death angels will pass you
By.
But the ending to Moses after he got
Started

And the pillar of fire and the red sea was
Parted
He didn't enter the promised land ...why?
Because of his temper he had to pass it
By.
So when you wish to be used of the lord
And you feel you have sins that weigh more than a
Load
Do not run or bow out of act out of turn
From Moses and Aaron take heart and learn
You can do the Lord's will and such
If you don't run or pass our God Up.

Playing House

I was glad to visit my friend today
I took my four year old to her house to play
And when the two little girls got together?
Well was I in for an eye opener and better!
First of all I heard her girl say
"Let's get our dolls out and dress em, okay"
And then I heard my daughter quietly respond..
"Okay, sounds good but I'll be the mom"
She said "I'll have three kids the two babies and you…"
"But you'll be the babysitter of the one dressed in blue"
"Oh , okay" said the other flat
And then play commenced and that was that.
But all of a sudden we heard a sharp shrill
And dishes were breaking and the noise about killed
Both of our ears as we looked at each other…
Because that was not how we acted as mothers!
But the daughter spat out (the one who was mine)
"You go to your room until you can find!!!!"
"All of your socks and all of your shoes"
"It makes me so mad when you continue to lose"
"This little stuff and just look at this dress!"
"Why I think that you are nothing but a big mess!"
The words that stuck in my own head spoken by her
Were the ones "You are nothing…the rest was a blur…
And then before I could get that out of my brain
She was screaming some more and took off again..
"And whats even worse" She was sobbing now
Is the ways you don't put away things like your bath towel
And you leave everything in such a huge slop
Why where ever you take it off there it just drops!
She was out of control she was beside herself
And I hung my own head to hear her grasping to tell
Of just how it was at our house and sure
That I had not been all that patient with her.
When the other little girl who was playing the part
Of my little girls daughter and babysitter's aren't
Likely to express the ways she would feel

But this was just playing it wasn't for real
So she said "I thought I told you about your mouth"
"I am telling your father and now don't you pout!"
"What's more I will suggest a spanking or two."
"And we'll see who comes out winner between me and you
my mommy does the same thing too."
"But she doesn't get very far before daddy gets through."
And then she said, "From now on that's who I'll be
I am not babysitting anymore , I'm the daddy."
"Okay, okay, okay," my little girl said
"I guess I'll put these babies to bed."
And we two adults heard them scurrying around
Creating makeshift beds for the babies to lay down.
Then all of a sudden we heard her girl
Say in a deep voice and this make our stomachs swirl
"I quit my job today, I told my boss
He'd just have to forget it and it would be his loss."
"Because I was sick and tired of him
And wanted to spend more time at the gym
At the gym there was this beautiful lady...
And the cute pink outfits she wears drives me **crazy**
Why I think I could stare all day at her."
And then my friend's face showed her concern
But we let them continue we did not stop
Their play acting drama and the moment was dropped
But we two looked at **each** other real hard
And almost wished now they had played in the yard.
I had come face to face with my poor mothering
And she had to wonder where her husband had been
So between the two of us we sat still as a mouse
And realized there **we** were simply playing house.

Protecting Sheep with a Stone

David was going to turn 15 on his next birthday.
His father was always sending him to watch sheep. Big deal he thought
....sheep.
And then....
The afternoon when he least expected that bear....
He killed it with his slingshot and a stone.
It was a pretty good story to tell around the table that night.
He went on to celebrate his 16th birthday too and on that day his father
surprised him with a brand new slingshot.
So the next time a wild animal tried to drag a sheep away he killed
it too.
He became a crackerjack sling-shotter.

It wasn't long until the war broke out....
Itching to go he begged his father to let him carry food to his older
brothers.
His father gave in to the request and David was off.

Goliath of Gath.
Struck fear into a man.
But it ticked David off the way he mocked God.
"Isn't anyone sick of him runnin' his mouth?"
David asked?
He doesn't look much different than a bear .
With slingshot in hand David swung once twice three times and
By nightfall the giants head was
On a platter.
It was a pretty good story to tell around the table that night.

David faced other giants too. Giants that would end up dragging him
off
Like a sheep...
And he fell.
Almost had his head on a platter
Making good topic for conversation around the devil's table.

And yet God said "No".
He went to the brook
Took a rock
A cornerstone
And sent him
To David.
And by nightfall on Davids platter
Sitting on top of David's table
Was the head of his giant.
Defeated and
Dead.
Because you see David wasn't the only boy sent
To protect some sheep
With a stone.

Purses

Throughout one's life we find
A series of struggles and curses
And we keep plowing thoughtless and blind
Opening various purses

In our first purse we saw
Our children a gift and treasure
But then at the bottom a claw
Rips us apart with pleasure.

Our second purse is busy and loud
With life being a roller coaster
Laughing, crying, lonely in a crowd
Burnt up like toast in a toaster.

The third purse we open is true
The quiet and subtle type
Leaving us manipulated and blue
Not worth any of the hype.

Now we find ourselves standing
Holding our fourth and last purse
Both finally settled and landing
Both weathered, worn and thirst

We thrive on each others being
In the room or just standing by
Entertaining the idea of leaving?
We'd both cry for the rest of our lives.

For but once in a life does it happen
That two people fall in love
And it may not be in fashion
But it is blessed by the father above

So this last purse we will open
And the contents in the bag?
Leave us strong, fulfilled and hoping
For a lifetime of beauty and brag.

Now my advice to you
Is if you have a good purse
Is to keep it close be so true
For you'll have a life of great worth.

Ready Or Not Here I Come

One....
Two...
Three....
Ready or not here I come!
And those of us hiding hoped and shivered with anticipation of
whether we would reach base, and be home free before we were
caught.
We await his coming and the ironic part is:
That **base *is* our hiding place.**
God leaves no room for excuses.

We still play hide and seek with
False pride,
Money,
Power,
Sex,
Drugs,
Family name, or
Any other earthly pleasure
It will be exposed
We will not reach base no matter how long the counting goes on.
So ready or not here I come
And *based*
On that *base*
Will get us home free.

Room at the End

When Jesus was born in Bethlehem town
With all of those animals walking around.
There weren't any hotels where they could sleep
So he was laid in a manger and slept with the sheep.
And even then as I notice now
Jesus laid down his riches to take up with the
Cows.
And I gather from the story now as then.
There was room for them all
There at the end.

Yes there at the end
He gave His life
He laid himself down by the animals' side
There at the end we could all receive and all come to glory
If we'd only believe.

When Jesus walked from town to town.
The rumors and dust were flying around.
Everyone could be promised to see .
That He'd rise again He'd not stay dead or asleep..

He still laid his riches aside
He pointed the way to eternal life
Still calls the same now as then..
Calls us to love to be brothers
And friends.

For you see ....

There in the end He gave His life. He laid himself down by the animals'
side. There in the end we all could receive
And all come to glory.
If we'd only believe...

I can see it all now
If He started out with the sheep and the cows.
He ended His life the same way then…
Surrounded by animals He considered His friends.
And when heaven we know is just round the bend…
Remember… oh yes know…
There's room at the end.

Rugs

I wish you knew how sorry I am
For taking our love
For taking our trust
And shaking them out
Like rugs
Like last fall's rugs.
I took those rugs and
Shook them
Over the back porch banister.
And I wonder...
Has
That poor use and abuse of
Trust
And
Love
Set into motion your defense system.
Because when I am done in the back...
You take the rugs
And head to the front.
And then around and around
And around the house ....
We go....
Shaking rugs.
Picking the things up left and right.
I want to lay those beautiful rugs
Down and let them serve their
Purpose.
Or maybe carpet
Or hard wood
Then
We can look at each other and say...
We do not have anything else to shake
Over the back porch.
And if we do ....
Well it wont be our
Rugs.

Runaway Quarters

There he lay been there for almost 20 years...
Begging outside the city gates.
Life had trickled down to nothing
And everyday the same town prostitutes
Coming into the city would toss him a coin or two.
He had become an expert at catching them
And unless some rolled out of reach....
He'd have quite a stash by the end of the day.
He laid there lowly and unnoticeable

But when it was announced that the teacher was coming through
Well he took heart.
Maybe Jesus would notice him.
Maybe he will see me as he walks through the gates...
And he did...
And so when Jesus came to his own town some men came to get
The paralytic lying on a mat and upon seeing their faith Jesus said..
"Take heart son your sins are forgiven"
"Get your mat and go home"
The lame man was whole.
Ready to be able to work
To have a family and children too.

But the bible never goes back to find out how he did..
It may have been something like this....

"Ya know" said the healed lame man "This walking to work has worn
me out"
For five years now I have trudged through the weather and the dirt.
My wife is a nag and the kids are a nuisance...why I remember when I
was on that
Mat...
Life was so simple...

And I think of myself.
I trade out lameness for blindness
Deafness for death all the time...

And I shouldn't get too carried away with
The rolling up my mat part and walking
Because it was just yesterday that
I was on the outskirts of town trying to catch
Runaway quarters.

Scared to Death

I have always wondered what death was like
Actually that is a lie
I have been so busy living
I have never imagined dying

I have been so self absorbed in
The beauty of my various jackets
That the option of what to wear
Took priority over caskets

I have been too busy running
My cars and motoring my mouth as well
That to stop and ponder heaven?
I haven't and would never tell.

So when I finally brought my
Self and pride to halt
And I began to see my friends
And all the stuff we'd bought

It did not hit me really
Until the hole in the ground was made
For my best friend's son in law
Died the other day.

And you should have heard the mourning
Oh my goodness the fury at the loss...
For the man in the ground they're sure
Had never heard of Jesus' death on the cross-.

And here I am boldly pouting and running
Life with haphazard uncertain
Not giving a minute to the profound
Reality of dropping the final curtain.

So today as I sit here thinking
I want to sell all my clothes.
For now I see that death is
Just a place our body goes.

If we make our days
A new blessing with each breath
Then my friend the dying
Won't be scaring us to death.

Seeing, Eye God

Today we went to the doctor
The one who helps people
See
And when the man looked at our glasses...
He looked between my husband and
Me..
"I cant believe you see anything "
Was what he said under his
Breath...
"For these lenses are worn out and wobbly to boot you have
Practically worn them to
Death"
My husband being the man
The man of pride that he
Is
Said"Well doc just two months ago I underwent surgery for
This"
"Oh said the eye doctor puzzled
And we saw the alert in his
Eyes
You can see clearly now but still need glasses"
I cant help but feel very
Surprised"
And we sat and at him
Just stared
Neither of us knew what to
Say
Both of us seeing
Impaired
Had glasses and couldn't see
Anyway !
For you know it could be you've
Toiled and maybe fought hard all of your life
And even though you think you see clearly
You cant bring your own heart into
Sight.
For trust me my friend and my

Brother
And trust me when I say this to
You
We all have to see as the lord
Does
And he looks at us from blood shed that's
True.
He could not ever see anyone if on their own they stayed
So with his life and death on a cross he willingly paid.
And even though we still can not
See our sins our faults and are
Blind
He doesn't see them either now
For we stand close and hide
Behind
The torturous instrument used long ago the one that sets us all
Free
It is like the knife that corrected his sight
Cutting us all loose to
See.
So I call him the seeing eye God
I call him father of all wonder on
High
For He in His wisdom and mercy
Gave us the ability to regain our
Sight.

She Would Settle

Her parents lived in a trailer court all of her life.
So she was raised up with next to nothin.
They were clean and well behaved. But when it came time to draw her
dream house for that school art project?
She wanted to draw a castle sprawled out over the countryside with
green wavy grass and rich purple heather.
But she settled for a simple drawing of her trailer court
Sandwiched on both sides by double wides.

She finished her school years and it came time to choose some sort of
group to run with. Since she was used to being common she settled
for the two girls down the row. They weren't going to college. So she
settled for that burger bob job too.

Years passed and it came time when guys and gals start looking
around planning a mate...planning a future. By now she had settled for
the common so...she went with the boy from burger bob. He was okay.

More years and more and then came time to choose neighborhoods
and schools for their children. She was willing to do what had come
natural.... Settle. But one day...

The preacher from the first baptist church called. Said he would like
she and her husband to enroll their children in the church school.
It was brand new, had great teachers and it was going to be full of
activities. They enrolled their children in school and even ended up
joining the fellowship.
She settled into the women's bible study and Wednesday night prayer
meeting. She made new friends and eventually took classes on line to
earn a little business degree. Her husband had become co owner of
burger bob and they were opening two more restaurants across town.
But it wasn't until that particular Friday that she saw...really saw how
much Christ had changed her life.
There was an art contest at school.... Draw your dream house...and
Her daughter took first prize with the picture of a castle.

Sometimes Late at Night

My mind just goes crazy
With thoughts of my past.
I lay there wide awake for hours and hours
Watching 2:30 then 3:30 come and go....
I can't imagine how I could have lived that way and how
I could have done to you what I did.
And people when they read this
Will each think
I am talking about them.
But it broke your heart to see me squander my money
To run after pig's food as a child of God.
And it I know caused you such anguish to see the people that
I bruised and abused through it all
And I know that only
You are able to repair them
To mend them and to heal
I know that the times I sold my own blood for gas and for food you
could relate because
You shed yours
For me on a cross and that cost you your life.
I watch as if I were a yacht plowing through the ocean
The wake
As
It comes back together slapping hard on the shore
And I know within my heart
That it is consequence for sin coming back to the shores of my life over
and over and over again.
Finally it eases though
You have seen enough
Because you ...you have also been awake late at night
Watching the hours come and go...
Going crazy with the thoughts of what I would one day become
And knowing what you did for me would be enough
Yes
More than enough to work through me.
And now I sometimes lay awake at night for hours and hours
Knowing you are
Up at night watching over me going crazy with love for my soul.

Sooner

"I wish I had met him sooner." she thought to herself.
If she had, she would have missed all the rocks and potholes.
"Really" she thought, "They were boulders, tremendous mountains and
Deep chiseled caverns." "Gorges and rocky eroded canyons."
If she would have met him sooner she would have missed all the pain.
The steady stream of rumors and the ruining of not only her
reputation
But the trust of her only son.

And they looked at the Christ and said,
"If you had come sooner our brother, Lazarus would not have died."
"It took you three days longer ---why he's already dead and buried."
"He stinks!"
But Christ walked into that room of hateful death and
Called his friend back to life...to light ...to health...
To himself.

So you see now don't you?
That if he had come sooner
You may not have needed him to come at all.
Faith is now a ladder that allows for the climbing over any rocky
mount.
Mercy, grace and trust are ropes of absolute knowing that you will
Swing over the potholes.
The cross bridges the weedy canyons and closes up the death gorge.
But if he had come sooner
You and Lazarus wouldn't have died.
Where"s the glory in that?

It'd still be lying in the bottom of a canyon somewhere.

Spitting Cobras

The man and wife were in bed----
Blood draining scream---
Hooded figure
Weaving swaying
Piercing eyes trained dead center
On her ...a spitting cobra..

It was his gambling problem.

The computer expert never saw
The cougar slash out his throat
Leave him bleeding
And it was his porn addiction all along.

The man's boss was strung up by his ankles in a tree and
He never saw the bear hovering close
The bear of lies.

Remember the coworker
Who used to manage the money for your
Company?
Found his carcass picked to death by
Vultures...of infidelity

Have you looked in the mirror lately?
Your arms have cuts and serious razor
Sharp canyons dug into them...
Canyons of deep pride.

What would happen if we saw our problems
Our sins as animals...
How far would we go before we took action?

How many nights would we snuggle up
In bed

With a spitting cobra...not too many
Before we would become blind..
And that is how we have become to our compulsive gambling
Blind.

And would we actually say
"Here kitty kitty" to a cougar?
Come slash our throats ?
But that is exactly what our porn problem is
Doing to us.

And would we just walk straight up to a bear and tickle him
Under the chin
Provoking a stringing up?
Our lies are doing that to u s too
Stringing us up .

The man who has infidelity in his life?

Is that him bragging about hanging out with
Vultures?
He picked them as friends and now they have picked him back..
To death.

Then there we are with those cuts on our arms..
The talons of pride have left us bleeding and
Cut up...

So if sin were an animal?
I'd go on a hunt ....
And I would start by hunting spitting cobras.

Staying Babies

I met a grownup the other day
Had to be forty or so I'd say
But had his thumb stuck in his mouth
And a diaper trailing out

So I asked him "What of this?"
As his mommy bent to kiss
And knew it „not just maybe
That he'd stayed a little baby.

His whole world, yes his whole life
Centered around three kids and wife
And pacifiers, windup toys and rattles
Cheating, lying running to tattle

Couldn't take him anywhere
His dinner manners poor, I swear!
And needed to be in a pen to play
Because he still acted like a babe.

His pants he'd wet with excitement and
Sometimes he'd remove his wedding band
When the pressure would get too tight
Or when his diaper didn't fit just right.

Yes when things wouldn't go his way
He'd pitch one of his fits and say
"I don't need anyone of you!"
But down deep inside he knew the truth.

He was not a grownup man yet
And no matter how bad things get
His plan would never change
Unless they be suited for a rearrange

Then one day he went to school
He had a teacher who went by the rules
And the standards were very high
It made the man so mad he cried

"I just don't want it to be this way!"
"I want to go outside to play!"
But his wife kept him there, said"dear"
You need to stay at least a year.

So as the year went by so slow
The man began to sprout and grow
New ideas and new thoughts too
He began to see the people who

Had to put up with him in life
And then starting with the first,,,his wife
He began to make things good
And he slowed down and took

Time to be a friend to her
And not just a man she'd have to burp
He realized he'd had damaged and
Would have to start acting like a man

And with the three kids they were next
He started leading and doing his best
He began to think that almost maybe
He had stopped being like a baby.

At work, at church and especially home
When it would be his eyes to roam
And tempers to flare and tantrums pitch
He'd stop and consider which..
Voice it was he was listening too
The baby one or the teacher's who

Taught him how to use a fork and knife
Told him how he'd saved his life
And his all upon a cross he laid
To he would not have to stay a babe

And we all are in this boat
With pacifiers and bibs round throats
And think we walk when really all
We do is giggle, cry and crawl

So the next time God on high
Says to be quiet and stop the crying
He expects more out of us yep maybe
He is tired of us staying babies.

Stick with Gum

She came through the church doors
Like spring wind
Like early mist
Like new snow
And she sat toward the back with her legs crossed and a hat on her
head
In the middle of the choirs song she removed
Her hat.
She must have known that song because
There from the back she belted it out!
Yes she stood up and sang right along with the
Choir
The entire congregation on cue turned to look.
With pink in her cheeks she sat down.
After the choir filed out the collection plate was passed.
As it crossed her lap she loudly blurted
"Oh you generous people"
But not a dime did she give.
When the preacher took the podium
She began fumbling around in her purse.
Maybe she is looking for her bible
Or perhaps a pen.
But when she pulled out a bright yellow pepper?
And she chewed like a surly old cow?
Well the preacher had his hands full trying to regain control.
How like the typical church goer is that?
Sweeping into church competing with the choir
Commenting on the money
And although we don't chew on peppers?
If sin could be seen I imagine it would
Be like bringing in a big ol yellow pepper and chomping down.

And you know?
If sin were that obvious?
We would hum along with the choir
Give a tenth to the bowl
And just stick with gum.

Still Moving

The bible lay motionless on the counter
But on the inside Christ was
Standing…
Walking…running
Climbing, skipping
Swimming, roaming,,
Searching, hoping
Fishing, thanking
Healing, bathing
Calming, soothing
Sacrificing, battling
Praying, singing
Entering, protecting
Interceding, warning
Restoring, promising
Forgiving,
Telling, feeding
Shouting, whispering
Watering
Growing, feasting
Partying, loving
And the whole time the book lay motionless.
Must have been the part when he was dying.
But then he
Arose
Ascended
Now seated.
Soon he'll stand

Then the rest of all man kind
Will…
Kneel,
Confess
Weep
Hide
Faint
Worship

Sing
Awaken
Laugh
Listen

And
Some will
Perish.

And we can shut the book up tight
Lay it high on top of our closet shelf
It can gather dust until next Easter rolls around.
But he is
Still moving.

Stopping Traffic

Today we saw an interesting
sight...
A man in the middle of a busy
Highway
And what he was doing took us a minute to
Tell
He was bustling around to pick up something that
Fell
They were pieces from his toolkit pieces
Of tools
And evidently they were things he did not want to
Lose...
For he had stopped traffic both coming and
Going
And we were all waiting wondering and loudly
Groaning.
Finally he had all of his
Kit
And when the lights turned to green
Feet began to pick up
And lift.
But there was one more item still stuck in the
Road...
And the man held up one finger
Right close to his nose
Held all cars and vans yes he held them all
Up
And quickly scooped the last of his kit in the
Truck.
I watched this and smiled to
Myself
How like the savior is that ?
He's my greatest wealth.
He's the reason I am inside the box
He's the reason I'm
In
He was the one who stopped for me to be

Friend
So as I watched the man drive away...
I thought thank you lord you
Have lessons to teach me each
Day
But as we drove by his green truck I suppose
He'll never think there's a connection between what he did,
And the Lord

Tall Tales

A man with long hair and that's his strength
Walking around Jericho taking great lengths
To not say a word?
Not make a move ?
Not discuss strategies
Not try to prove?

Or

How about bumble bees winning a war?
Or loaves of bread from oil in one jar?
Laying atop the dead to bring back life?
Gaining heaven by losing your life?
Dying to self so you may live?
Giving to gain or after a drought rain rain rain.

And

Feeding 5000 with two loaves and five fish
Sending a damaged skin in the Jordan to dip
Not once or twice but seven times now
And on that seventh time clean how?
Putting mud on blind eyes to see
And raising the dead from across the sea.

Or

Calling fishermen to serve a king
Letting shepherds know the birth before anything!
Coming as a humble newborn babe?
Staying the same age after age?
Freeing the prisoner
Taming the wild
To become like him is to be a child

And

Rivers of blood
A forty day flood
Lions laying down with the lamb
The meal with the taxman
The prostitutes washing feet
A word to all he meets

Rose again on the third day
Will come in the clouds not too far away

So many examples of unbelievable stuff
And living holy can sure be rough
Trusting in someone we cant see
Is where we are finally eternally free.

The Ten Unspoken Prayers

Every single Sunday when we go around the class
And we each woman a prayer request we ask....

Lift up my family as we travel from here to there...
And health, and about our country and the ten unspoken prayers...

And no one but the lord above, knows, or sings or shouts
But last week I wondered cause' this' what came about...

The community garden fed 1000 souls
And old Mrs. Tilman went to meet the lord....

The freshman youth in college passed her first biology test,
And the Beckman's brought their new baby home together with the rest.

The choir sang in tune a song they had not practiced...
Because brother Tim spent the week traveling safely back to us.

Gloria got remarried to a great christian man ocean side
And her aged mother saw her happy right before she died.

Susan doesn't have leukemia, and the West Nile flu
Missed brother Oleand's niece and son who live up in Duluth.

And today I sit here puzzled and look at all the hearts we bear...
Hoping for another week of ten unspoken prayers.

The Bride of Christ

Wedding vows have always been
For women as brides and husbands

And the vows go something like this
When a couple enters into marriage bliss:

I take thee as my beloved spouse
And before God we'll set up house...

I vow to be forever true
And faithful in all that I do

Forsaking all others I will
Live with you lovingly until

Death comes and takes me away
So I abide with you until that day

Bestow all my worldly goods
In sickness and health abundance of food

Or in poverty and misery
From my heart I promise thee...

And then the man says basically
The same words to her and he

Puts a ring on her finger
There is a kiss and they linger

They stand before the room
As the wedded bride and groom

But have you ever wondered how
The child of Christ repeats their vows?

"I take thee Christ as my savior
And I will try to not waiver"

But invite you into this heart of mine
You can have most of it and that's just fine...

I won't promise you I'll forsake
Because now on Sundays there is the game....

And be faithful to you for richer or poorer?
Are you sure I have to do that chore?

I mean good grief ho hum come in ..welcome
Sit down in my chair?
You want to clean where?
Oh so you think you know?
The places I now can't go?
And you are changing all my friends?
My patience now has reached the end....
I have not even been given a ring
In fact I have not been given anything....

Till death do us part? Yeah right that's it!
I want a divorce! Right now..I quit!!!

And Christ the honorable husband he is
Slides the ring of son-ship off that hand of his

And promises that in his death
He saved her forever and each breath...

She can be certain he has forsaken
All others and now has taken

Her hand and soul into his own
And she is honored at his throne..

So then she hangs her head
And he hangs too for her instead...

That by his death on the cross
She is redeemed ...it's satan's loss.

She sees that she has new life
As she is now the bride of Christ.

The Bump in the Rug

I saw in the book there was a man who took
For himself gold and silver and
Fine robes.
He hid them in the ground under his tent.
He was a warrior .
He had helped defeat
Jericho.
The walls to that city fell to them
With a few trumpets blasting and a couple of
Loud yells.
So when they lost the
Battle to a much smaller foe in the
Next go around?
Well Joshua began looking.
He lined them all up and asked them one question.
"What are you hiding"
Finally the poor guy fessed up.
They had sin in their camp.
Hidden sin.
And to take care of it they put him
And his family to death.
Then they defeated the small enemy with no trouble.
I can't help but think of my own life.
I rise up in the strength of the
Lord God
And defeat an enemy that would ordinarily
Devour me.
It seems like such
An easy win that I take
Just a little credit for myself.
After all I surely had something to do
With it.
But the next day when I fall miserably
To a much smaller issue?
I am shocked!
Why won't God bless me?
I am working so hard!

I am trying so hard!
I look around until my head spins off
But God is not in it.
There in the floor of my heart is a bump in my rug.
I have a cloak of pride hidden
Buried down deep.
Along with a sheckle of selfishness and three or four pounds of
Greed, arrogance, and critical fault finding.
Because after all...
As long as I can keep my eyes searching for everyone else' sins
And locating everyone else' struggles?
Raise my eyebrows and point fingers at the ways they
Dress
Behave
Raise their kids
And spend their money....
Mine stay
Untouched
Buried safely
Guarded with my watchdog
Of defensive pride
And I don't get the victory.
Not until I step out into the clearing and shake
The rug.
I let God put that stuff to death.
I can ooooh and aaaah over the sins
In others
But the battle will never be mine
It can't.
That is why I defeat the big guys and lose to the small
I know I need him completely for the first. But the second time
around?
I take the credit and add it to my stash.
Then
I trip.
I trip over that stupid rug.

The Devil's Mercy

Today a flatbed semi truck cruised through
Town..
He obeyed the laws
He minded the speed
But when he swerved out of the way far
And wide?
I hung back
To see
To see what he wanted to miss
To see what it was that this
Beast could not take on...
And to my surprise it was a
Little
Dead
Squirrel.
So ...to the back slidden
To those Christians
Who are dead
The devil
Doesn't hit you anymore
You
Are
Already
Dead.
You are just a fistful of bones
And fur
And when you think about it like
That ?
I guess that is the devil's way
He shows
His mercy
Too.

The Map

The old man held the three year old little boy on his knee. He looked at him solemnly and said,"you are my great grandson, Matthew." "I have in my hands a map which I am going to give you today."

"Throughout the ages of man folks have desired a map...a daily guide..a course of direction ...you know a day by day 'what-to-do' thing."

"So Matthew, here you go."

The older gent handed the child a thick bound leather book...it was so heavy the three year old did not have strength to carry it.

Matthew's mother had just come in and she encouraged Matthew to get his toys and clean up so they could get back to their house...a storm was coming in and she wanted to secure things.

Once they reached the house Matthew's mom found the leather book and deciding it too 'grown up' and too heavy, she put the book up high on the tip top shelf in her closet. She did not want her three year old being burdened down with a book like that ....it didn't even have pictures.

Matthew forgot all about the book for years and years...

Toward the end of April, of this particular year, great grandfather was turning ninety two. The family was throwing him a big fan fare with music and food and some of them were planning on dancing. When Matthew drove up he saw his great grandfather sitting in the 'kings' chair right in the middle of everyone. Matthew walked over to the man and pulled up a folding chair...."Hey how ya doing ??" He asked.

Without replying to the question his great grandfather said, " I have to ask you Matthew ..did you ever look at the map ..the big leather book I gave you when you were three."

"I forgot all about it" said the kid and truthfully Gramps who could write a map to a life?" " I mean really ..mom said it would be a sweet keepsake and we just left it at that."

"go get the book." Said Gramps.

Go get it."

Matthew shrugged his shoulders in an effort to please the old man he loved so much and went to the closet . He could reach it easily.

He sat down on his mother's bed...just thumbing through the pages..

It began on the day he had given it back on march 4th 1963...Matthew was three and now it was 1983. Whew....

Matthew flipped through the first few pages....he read....

'March 17th 1967....it read...
When mom took the side of Bobby Croom instead of yours for the broken sliding glass door....you need to remember taking sides in a dispute doesn't mean taking sides against **you.**
Oh my thought Matthew....
This is crazy...thought Matt...Bobby Croom ..... Bobby Croom....wow he's in the army now..went in when his momma passed away...wonder how he's doing...

Then he read about the December 8th 1970 he was ten and the incident with Jill Maher. Respecting girls had been a theme for study in history class....they had been discussing in the fifth grade all about the roles girls played in the united states....Jill Maher was handicapped...stuck in a wheel chair she was wheeled into their classroom for history and art. She was skinny and frail and she would sling paint all around and then with real jerky motions she would try to talk.....he had made the mistake of asking what contributions could this girl ever make?
It made him cry even now remembering the whole conflict. It replayed in his mind vividly as if he were actually reliving it. Jill never grew up and she never got to dance at the prom....never had a boyfriend or a date ... did not have a job or a car and she never knew anything of babies or motherhood....she was gone. And she lived only twelve years.....she had not contributed anything....or had she...? There next to the date of February 2,1972 was the newspaper clipping of her obituary. _Local School Girl Passes to Glory_
It read....and he read how she met with other teens in the gym for prayer...and how she established the first "art rolls" club she combined a person in a wheelchair with a walking person to be teams in art .....she was the one who got the flowers planted around the flagpole and now there is a memorial covered year round with flowers to honor and remember her.
Women contribute so much....they are the foundation of our lives... they raise the children...they are our nurturers and lovers...they pick us up when we hurt ..dust us off and send us back out to the fight... and this girl this little Jill? Know the prayers the art pictures and the flowers all have done just that. They have sent hundreds even thousands possibly, back to the fight of life.
Matthew looked up not noticing he had been sitting on the bed for a

half hour or so. He took the book to his Great Granddaddy...they were still dancing and singing ..but Gramps was cutting the cake, getting ready to blow out candles...he closed his eyes tightly and mumbled his wish... Then he hugged Matthew close...read the rest he whispered... Read the rest....

When he sat down later that week he read all about his life up to the age he was presently. He read about failing the science exam in advanced biology because he cheated...he read the part about having to enroll again and...

This was where he stopped.....the things written next would be his future...his destiny ...written here on the next few lines would tell him what to say..which road to pursue. Mother did not know he had been kicked out..and she had no idea of him cheating later that week he had an appointment to appear before the board of directors who determined whether or not his college career should continue.

He sat there. Stunned and let his eyes move to the next sentence and the next.

When they asked him why he thought they should let him come back to finish his undergraduate degree...he remembered saying

"I have this great gradfather ,,,see."

He went to this college and his daughter went and my mom went and I chose this university to carry on the tradition...."

"Seems like a feeble answer" he said "But there was also this girl in my fifth grade class named Jill ...Jill Maher"

She was in a wheelchair all of her life...and when she passed away the school put this memorial by the flag pole ."

"I guess I went to college to finish something for her...since she did not get the chance.."

And tears began building up in his eyes...what he did not know was the chairman was also getting teary...he said...

"Matthew farmer...that little girl was my great granddaughter..Jill, Jill Maher."

And he put down his pen and said "If it is possible could you be back in school to finish your education and degree in advanced biology Monday?"

Matthew did.

And....when he had the chance to walk across the stage to graduate...he instead was wheeled across in honor of Jill and her Great Grandfather who let him come back....

That map ended up not just being a path for his future but a gift of insight to loving others along the way...
Matthew ended up marrying a young woman from the biology lab.
They had a daughter and Matthew named her Jill.

Mr. Maher never lost contact with Matt, and when his Matthew's own dear Great Grandaddy died in the fall of 1986?
Matthew buried the map with him...
And a note tucked inside the book that read
"Thank you Great Grandfather for this Bible...it has been a lamp unto my feet and a light unto my path.

Love, Matthew

The Winter of 73

It was the coldest winter of my life. I was six and my mom had taken all six of us to Woolco to buy boots, hats and gloves. They were picking out camouflaged stuff and my mom was picking toy train baby mittens for me. I hated them. I remember as if it were yesterday the shrill yelp of delight from my oldest sister Gloria. She pushed her way to where I stood and said ,"Sam, hey Sam...look at what I found you." I looked up and saw the coolest mittens ever. They were green and muddied brown. Plush and soft, warm and tough looking...I loved them and I wanted them. When I saw the price and it said they were five dollars... my hopes fell. I just knew mom would never buy them. But at the register she shuffled the groceries in with the snow gear and on we went. I found them by my pillow the next morning. Oh was it a grand entrance coming in from the bus. I swung my arms way out like a fancy Canadian soldier trying hard to let the teachers see my new mittens. Recess couldn't come soon enough and the minute the bell rang I was out and running. I shot off like a bullet to get the girls and just as I tagged the girl from Mrs. Gentry's class she twisted her coat sleeve out of my grip and my beloved right mitten came off! The return bell was sounding and in we all went. I could have cried. I wanted to go back out and find the mitten. What would mother say? Just one day one day! I sobbed down deep and walked away never finding that mitten. That was thirty three years ago. Seems funny about life and what we consider important....but after college I married my high school love and we moved back to my home town. I was actually teaching in the same classroom as when I was a little guy. One day I had a project I wanted to show the kids. I had never had time to pull the papers and paints from the three shelves above the sink. I sent one of my more responsible students to bring me the boxes. She skipped over to them and began saying ,"ahhhh" "look at this ..it's so cute." What? I asked well she said there is a mitten in here with a note...says "hold for Sam..he'll be back." Who's Sam she asked?
I was unable to hold back those memories. There in perfect teacher print was my name. I thought of all the years and all the times I felt the loss of the little mitten. I carried it home and eventually had it framed. I loved the mitten for it was a symbol of happy days and those are things to be treasured for sure.

The Selfishness of Suffering

Most of the time really straight and narrow types of Christians,
You know the kind I'm talking about..
The ones that sing in choirs
And
Teach Sunday school
And
Chalk up their giving tally's like maybe they are the only ones doing it...
Yea them...
Well they are the ones that will embrace suffering for a minute.
Their grandmother is ill,
Or they know of someone with cancer
Or perhaps there is a teen who is on drugs
Someone might be pregnant
Or not pregnant anymore..
And that is their idea of suffering....
And it better not last past the hip replacement surgery
Or the radiation
Or the juvenile correction
Or the crisis center outreach...
It just better not.
If it does then people will start judging faith..
and they'll cup hands around mouths
And they will whisper
And look at you
Then look away real quick.
So what do we do if the granny dies
And the cancer friends do too
And the teen runs?
What do we tell friends?
What do we tell God?
Most of us get mad.
How dare He not listen?
How dare He not move and jump and run when we say?
and why do our words not impress Jehovah?
He is not a puppet nor a dog nor is He some hopping lettuce eating long eared rabbit we pull out of a tall hat to please and wow a crowd.

He is in the crowd.

Front row. Center seat. Sitting just as still as a white dove.

He waits for our one man show to be over then he pulls us to the side and says...

If she lives ten more years your son will stay lost for twenty more.

And if I remove cancer from her or him they are going to end up divorced because the wife is cheating on him and she is going to break the entire family apart then the uncle on your mom's side won't end up going to seminary because of this witness ...

And God gets all hunkered down and says and you know something? They are already mine. But the ones they bring to life through their death aren't..

So uh..how bout lettin' me take over from here?

And the granny passes

And the cancer gets worse ..

The teens are locked up and the pregnant girls' deliver

And many many oh so many come to know Him as Lord and King and Ruler.

The next time you raise a petition to the King..

And you see things getting worse..

And then really bad...

Don't give up or in

And don't go raising fists to the skies...

Think of how many will come to the throne

And when they do

They find you there surrendered and checking yourself

Instead of boxes...

Accepting the fact that suffering is a part of identification

And you will have good measure of that too...

Oh yes you will...

Selfishly speaking.

Smell of Sin

The poor thing had soiled herself earlier in the car coming over to the counseling clinic and the smell? Well the smell was outrageous and every nose was alarmed while every eyebrow raised. Surely a woman knew better than to do this. Surely. The counselors literally held their breath to see who would have to sit across from this smelly raunchy mess. So when she sat down in front of me, I thought to myself "of course there was no other choice!" "It had to be me ….I get 'em all!"

But through the problems of her home life and through the issues of losing her job and her health taking a dive, and of course the awful smell….she began to sense something. A very profound feeling came over her and her eyes got big and then bigger and then she began to cry. Not just a little feminine cry like all women have from time to time…no she began to wail…she was hanging her head and shaking it back and forth and the smell was being stirred up and the room was filling with noise and with the rank odor. She realized her sin. She confessed it all and asked Christ to come into her life. Slowly she lifted her head and smiled at me. She thanked me for sharing the love and mercy of Christ. I admit I was rather glad to see her go and the room did not clear out from the terrifying smell of human for at least an hour.

Then Christ told them….you do not realize that you are naked wretched, poor and blind. He nailed me to a "t" with my pride. And he nailed it on the nose with my arrogance. Because unbeknownst to all of us I used to go around in dirty smelly soiled pants too. I, too would enter a room and without realizing it he'd hold his breath. He'd hold his tongue from voicing the truth about the sin smell. I see it all now so clearly. She was just more honest and real about it was all. Could not hide the fact she had messed herself up, the proof was too real. Without any obvious proof I smelled too. Only I believe I would have come to the holy lord much quicker had I smelled the sin I was sitting in…

The Trick

The trickster came to our town
I thought he was just fooling around
Made water turn right into wine
Healed those who once were blind...
We were impressed as he went through the door
But I followed him home then I saw more.

He took off his mask and there underneath
Was gnarled red skin and yellowish teeth
And in his hands he had a ball
That told who still stood and who had fallen
He had a cup of the wine he'd made
And instead of red...it smoked a gray shade
And he chugged it down and down it went
But he turned around my presence he sensed.

He did not fee feee fi fo fum at all
No, across his face a smile crawled..
I sat there in the darkness shaking
As I saw the measures this guy was taking...
He had a girl with in his grasp..
He would touch her and she would laugh
He threw her up into the air
And caught her with his fist in her hair..
He confused her about her worth and then
He turned her loose to walk among men.

For the guys who looked on her with scorn
They beat her and molested her till she was torn
And then when she would try to hide
They ganged up to kill her..yes they tried.
And I just sat there in wild shock
Because then the guys saw a bunch of rocks..
And while the girl in torn clothes lay
In the dirt on that hot summer day
The trickster was going to finish her off...
But the scene was interrupted by the son of God..

He had known about the sin
And he had made a way for them
But he's a gentleman and will not force
Anybody to follow him ..it's a choice...
So while this girl lay in a heap
And the men were going to cause her deep
Pain and sickness that's for sure..
They hadn't counted on meeting the lord.

The trickster will be all about lies
He will make you think you are so wise
And he will cause you to be deceived
And miss Jesus' atonement and not believe...
That there is any help around...
That you're all alone laying on the ground
But if you'll look up into the clouds
He is saying softly to the crowds...
"Go in peace your faith today
Has set you free and there is a way
Not known to any other soul
How to be saved and healed and whole."
He then took the satan tricking machine
And he saw the scum and fire from his lips seethe
And he threw him into the lake of acid
And said to him "It's forever lasting"
While those around were looking on
Someone from the shore started a song
And it began to rise soft and slow
Rescue the perishing ..began to grow
And I'll tell you this in that moment
It was the strangest thing I'll admit...
But the creature satan bobbed up to
The top of the acid lake screaming those who
Had followed him and had done his bidding
He was laughing and hot and not a bit kidding..
He choked on his spit
And he slid underneath
He was not fit
To trick us test our beliefs...

And on the surface of the whole scene
I saw Christ Jesus He was gathering
All the wounded all the lost
All the blind, those who spent and all it'd cost
He picked them up and he held them close
He bound their sores he is God the Father, Son and Holy Ghost...
And when I realized that then
Satan lies and waits for men
He shows them the stuff that will make them great
But all it leads to in the end is hate
So when you are tempted to be perverse
Or follow the enemy and live under a curse...
Remember that he has a hold on you
He'll try to kill you before he's through.
So trust me my friends and listen close...
Satan didn't die nor from a grave arose.
He will never shed his blood for you
You'll shed your own for him it's true
So when a trickster comes into your town
And his fake miracles raise up a doubt
Check with the word of God right then
And it will show you the way to be walking in.
A trickster came to our town today
And I knew it was satan right away
He still had some redskin sticking out
Of his mask for crying out loud.

The Visitors

Some visitors came to our house for a while today.
They ate with us and w e put on our best
We showed then a great time and had some good laughs.
By the end of the night we had them all drunk.
Told them all our dirty jokes and sent them on their way with
memories to cherish for a lifetime.
They did not make it home. Between being hooked on drugs and
having their own porn account.
It was worth it. They never knew it was our job to ruin them, their
marriages and work. Tarnish their reputations and they never guessed!
We figured it out long ago how weak they were. How capable of
believing lies they were.
We took full advantage and scammed them all. After all they were just
visitors they didn't really live here.
we showed them such stimulation and adventure they were convinced
the excitement here was okay. About to pour another round of drinks
and tell an even filthier joke but they were tired so they headed off to
bed.
Poor things didn't wake up till noon. We had them.
But with blurry eyes and wobbly legs they made ti to the front door.
"Where are you going?" We shouted you are in no condition to
leave"."No" they said slowly
"We are"
And we should have never stopped to visit."
"We are the visitors remember?"
As I sat there I clearly remember thinking how nice it would have
been to go with them. But not one of them mentioned where their
home was.

The Walking Dead

Beer tattoos bikes cussing filthy black feet and nasty fingernails
Babies with snotty noses walking around in only diapers
And others in car seats sitting around in the dirt.
A tent a car hamburgers and hotdogs on plates
On the hood
Grab a beer and search for the buns
Watch out for the baby and girls with tank
Tops on with sagging stretched out bellies
And absolutely no idea of how
Life could be.
And on top of it all
A thief rode away on bald tires
Headed out drugs foolin' around playing around
\\
Lost \\\\so\\\\lost
House stairs columns and furniture cars new clothes jewelry too and
clubs with wine and steaks eating out and suits shoes kids graduating
with honors...
Three car garage vaulted ceilings just picked up another rolex get your
nails done and a pedicure and a body wrap and a massage
And with all of this they without
Christ are just as lost
And remember don't get too far away from the memory of when you
were wandering around in the dirt like the
Walking dead
Because it wasn't that long ago and you know??
Cars
And
Clothes
And
Soap

Are the only
Difference..

And Then the Way

Walking .. The sun was shining all around
My feet were sure the path full of friends

And then the way .....
Crowded up a bit...bunching more than I could handle
I was tripping and almost falling bracing my hands on friends backs.....

And then the way .....
Was full of traps and stumps
Tangled roots and nets. I took off my party shoes

Running full speed now trying to catch up with the crowd that tripped me
I was tired, and thirsty ....I had not rested for weeks.

And then the way....
Shrouded down until I could not see any light
And I had to stop running and for sure I stood still ....lost.

And then the way.... Became darker....laughter echoed through the timbers
Wolves, and owls, serpents and spiders gathered ,spun webs and laid bare teeth...

And then the way....
Filled with mud and rain fell
Blurring my vision and I lost my direction and I fell too

Falling to my knees I groped for a strong tree trunk to hoist myself up with or to lean against.

And then the way ....
Was hoisted up for me
In the night sky I saw his body raised

And then the way ....died...........

Today I was reminded you are the life, and you are the truth.....
But most of all dear God ...
You are the
Way.

Weight of Sin

The weight of sin
Is a terrible thing
It takes out your jump
It removes your string
And it will destroy you
Concentrating
The weight of sin.

The weight of sin
Is a sure fire loss
It kills you joy
It controls and bosses
And in the end it will turn and toss
The weight of sin.

The weight of sin
Is hell bound for sure
No second chances there
Everything burns...
And the trouble is where
Oh ma'am and sir
It is the weight of sin.

The weight of sin is
Deceitfully quick
The whole ploy and game
Is to leave you tricked.

The Year That the Floods Came

I can remember the
Gardens getting drenched
At first we all thought it was a
Blessing and that our carrots
Would be bigger than ever...
That the peppers would be
Mild and the pumpkins and
Squash round and colorful
That never happened.
It was the worst spring.
Everyday it rained.

Not just a few minutes or even a few hours.
It rained solid for days.
And weeks..
And finally after a couple months.
It stopped.

And so did she.

She just up and quit.
Our neighbor's daughter
Had to come home from college early.
They said she had met up with a boy not
From their social class,
He had no money,
No family name,
He did not have a job,
His dad didn't even
Have a job...and they say she
"got pregnant".
The news traveled
Fast because right
When we opened our
Door to let the dog out..
There were terrible
Screams and cries

Coming from the house next to us.
My mother ran over to their house and banged on the door.
No one came to the door for a long long time.
My mom stayed there banging away and yelling,
"Margie, let me in." And yelling and banging...

Finally I'm peeking through the sheers
And the door opens and Margie our
Neighbor falls into my mother's arms.
She's screaming, "She's dead!"
"She's dead!" "My baby darling girl is dead."
and my mother cups Margie's face in her
Hands and they sit down hard on the step.
The life is gone from her eyes now.
And going to her house is like visiting a shrine.
And my mother whispers when we talk about the situation.

It was the year the floods came
It was the year that rain fell hard for months.
And nothing grew
Everything was pounded down.

And I thought about that today
Because there was a black man
To stop by their house.
He rapped on their door.
He looked around nervously
Trying to figure if he had the
Right place or not.
I stepped out on our front step
And motioned with my hand to
Get his attention.
When he looked around
I saw he had a baby gift tied
With yellow satin ribbon.
He came over to where I was
Sitting and asked, "You know
this girl dat live in dis house?"

Yes I replied
I did
Well he said

"I do be dat missionary
That has come for to
Carry her away to my country
And she is giving birth any day yes?"

"In my country it is not proper for
Man to see pregnant girl until
Date of delivery...and I??? Well
I been keeping track....so she
Is not home? I will come again..."
And he turned to go...

I called out
"Wait"
She is gone
She is dead.

His mouth fell open.
His present dropped
He collapsed and the floods
Came

And his tears rained down.
After what seemed to be a month or more
He tore himself away and scribbled a note...
Tucked it in the door jam. And shuffled back to his car.

What we all didn't know was that she had married him.
She was going to the mission field
She was happy and in love..

And blessed
And pouring out with showers of blessing

And her family only saw..
One thing...
That it was the year the floods came.

There's a Difference

There's a difference between a shout and a
Scream.

There's a difference between a wink and a
Blink.

And a difference between calling a girl and a
Call girl.

And a difference between light and being
Illuminated.

And there's a difference between being strict and being
Just stern.

There's a difference between driving and being
Driven

And a difference between calling and
Following one.

There's a difference between being a father and
Being a
Dad.

There's a difference between firing police and
Police firing

There's a difference between walking in the rain and
Walking on water.

There's a difference between light salt and
Being salt and light.

And

I wonder with all these differences if we even know the difference
Between gracefully saving
And saving
Grace?

Because the difference is as vast
As being cold and
Having
One.

They Aren't Mine

I have always wondered why it'd be
For me to judge others so tirelessly
And pick on everything they
Do
While I sit back and decide and choose
The ways that they dress to their pink hair
Baggy pants, pierced eyebrows I declare!
But the clothes they have are the product of
Very few praises sung and a lacking of love
They didn't think they could measure up
And from where I sit as I smirk?
Maybe its that I don't wear their shirt.
And what of this? I asked my friend
Your kids are a mess it is a sin
And she just hung her
Head
She did the best she could she said
But I knew I didn't understand this
How could a woman abandon her kids?
You see she'd had mother for twenty five years
With those wild parties,
Drugs and beer
Since it was her husband's
Mom
She felt she should support
And be calm
But as I saw her there as quiet as a mouse
She explained that I didn't live in her house.
And then my neighbor to my right
Has to be staying up late at night
Because their light is always on
So you know I thought something's wrong.
Today I decided to go over there
And to my surprise in a special chair
Was a girl couldn't have been
More than either nine or ten
And my neighbor was feeding her

Been up for nights the days were a blur
And then as she ran a brush through her hair
I could not stand to look at the girl in the chair.
It was not too long after all of that
I saw a lonely soul wandering down at the tracks
Had a beaten up face and nasty old clothes
I judged him quickly and turned up my nose
As I put the signal to go down main street
I saw the man looking down at his feet
And I saw then what he stood to lose
He was wearing his last pair of shoes
How totally ignorant yep totally wrong
For you to even be out here at all
Why you should at least be at a factory
Pulling good wages raising a family
Why in the world are you such a loser?
But what I didn't get was they weren't my shoes.
I pulled my car over to an empty lot
Bowed my head to thank our God
For surely this could have been me
Struggling and fighting every landing to reach
Life lived by others is different
And find
The chair, shoes, house and shirt are theirs
And not mine.

They Forgot Their Six Pack

There is a place where the fire dies not and the torment never ends and worms that never cease to eat away your flesh.....

Let's just take one of these ...how about the fire? It is the least scarey. After all maybe you have played with it for years. Maybe you know someone who has bravely started fires. Let me tell you there have been kids and adults say they'll just grab a six pack of beer, get a fishing pole for the worms... They'll sit down on the sulfur lake shore pop a top and make the most of it. But don't you see? Don't you understand anything about the devil? It's just like everything else he's tricked you to believe....fire can be managed....you are in control....don't believe Jesus He just doesn't want you to have fun with your friends, and he doesn't think you can control fire....He wants all the credit for being brave...I mean really dying on the cross...what an attention getter!

But

Just

Today after the fourth or fifth state burned out of control with wild fires...houses no longer stand. Dogs and cats fish, birds and game animals are simply gone...destruction and smoldering dreams lay charred and ashy....professionals not able in the least to control them. Hoses powders water chemicals dumped scattered pumped in drug in sprayed in or planned can't put the fires out....

People are certainly not grabbing fishing poles and hooking up canker worms. I did see a clip on TV of two teenagers running from the fire.... and I looked real hard at the screen but did not see any fishing poles and I thought to myself "Well honestly it came down to it on earth before hell ....you know they actually had a practice run, a freebie, a test drive to bravely face this raging storm of fury they so arrogantly have been deceived by satan who has made them think they can..... Golly, they must have forgotten their six pack.

Who They Bring

Of the seventy two people who board the bus
There are really 144
Of all who come on and sit
At least double walk through the door.

So the business man in stripes
Comes in with a grin
Faking confidence about his meeting
Because who came in with him.

He's brought his ego of frustration
Comparing how his boss is like
The man who adopted him
He still calls him 'Mike'.

Then there are the thousand memories
Of how his brother went to war
He feels the unneeded guilt
For his going away so far.

The bus is closing in
Approaching the convention hall
The man sitting across from him
Starts taking the time to call.

He, too, has more than just himself
Who is sitting in the seat
Paid the fare for himself
But two walked in off the street.

His wife has cancer
But he's having an affair
The purpose of this meeting
To promote his vision of software.

He sits with such anxieties
He is not sitting there alone.
He carries around the failures
He feels toward his son.

There's a woman who is despairing
She, too is accompanied then
By the thoughts of misused integrity
And her past abuse from men.

And there are fears that take shapes
Depression just pulled up a chair
Brothers blame and shame
Are sitting over there

There is sister expectation
Her older pal 'defeat'
Despair sits toward the back
And abuse took the front seat.

Abandonment finds rejection
Because they just hopped on
Standing rolling eyes and laughing
At a young mother and her son.

I am sure the bus driver
Never dreamed that he
Carries more folks than he thinks
All over the entire city.

But surprise of all surprises
The man who just boarded there
On the corner of trinity and third
Wearing sandals , and has long hair.

He just sat down
And I am sure they see
The unseen folks filing off
Running fearfully.

The evacuation is like a whirlwind
And this is strange but true
That despair just got up and left
And peace sits next to you.

Contentment replaces turmoil
Rest replaced mistrust
Smiles and honesty
Spreads over all of us.

And the beauty of his spirit
Isn't in the turning from
But in the willing confrontation
Of these demons and boldly come.

His voice stills wild storms
In the darkest nights he sings
He boards buses all over town
And chases out those extra ones we bring.

The meeting? It went terrific!
The affair? It had to stop.
The pasts of all of them
Are over and the pain is dropped.

Anxieties are vanquished
And birds flutter on their wing
The bus is lightened by at least half....
And just seats those who they bring.

Playin' Doctor

He spoke to the lowly
You crowd around the mighty...

He befriended the have not's
You'd have nothing of

He witnessed the dying ..
The fallen
As you walk by not noticing

He stooped to wash feet
As you step on toes....

With him there was silence
Until you with your clanging bells
And cymbals
Came along
All in the name
Of love

He fed the hungry
He bled for them too

You do similar things
You feed on and bleed people to death.

When he came to your town
The ones who saw him first
Were modern day shepherds and fishermen
The lowest of all
The worst.

They would be the oil field workers
And truck drivers
Not the doctors and such

But you missed him because he was
The doctor

There are some who would have seen him

They just pulled in a fresh catch
Of fish and
Delivered it to your door in a truck....

And you still don't get it
Because you are the one too busy playin' doctor!!!!

Too Many Rods

"No one can serve two masters...
He will choose one to hate.
And one to cling to.
He will despise one
And will love the other"

"There" he thought
I have made up my mind
I am not going to think about
That other woman again.
He put his pen down on his desk.
Out of routine more than anything else
He called his wife.
She picked up.
A pleasant voice she had
Pleasant.
She was busy at work
And he smiled thinking how simple it all was.
When he hung up
He saw the light
Blinking on his
Message machine
It was "her"
"Just one more time" and he dialed her back.
The voice on the other line
Sounded ...
Pleasant.
Had he dialed the wrong number?
"who is this" his wife was saying ...
"honey is this you?!" "who were you calling?"
It was a long ride home..
When he swung into the
Driveway he saw the
Curtains move.
"Honey I'm home!" "I'm home"
When he stepped into his bedroom
The woman there was not his wife

It was the other woman.
She clasped her arms around his neck
And said
"a realtor showed me this house today...
"She took me up on any offer."
And said in a very pleasant voice..
"enjoy"
"I'm so excited...what do you think?"
"Too many rods" thought the man
"Too many rods."

Too Much Like Life

Flat long strings of death.
That's how the scenes were in the movie.
Dark
Perverse
Obscene
Slanderous
Slaying
Venomous
What was meant to entertain
Was too much like life
And we do this to ourselves.
We bring in T.V., movies, radio, music and the like to help us escape
from our pain
Hate
Failures
And
Unfulfilled feelings we have in our marriages
Our kids
Work
Religion
And in
Us
And we are not refreshed
We don't leave the house
We don't go on vacation
For we have brought it home with us
And we laugh at the very things that do us in
We stare and listen to
The exact things that kill us.
And it is strange
For if we were needing release from it that badly?
Why would we
Pay to do it to ourselves?
In my opinion?
In my opinion
We are a bunch of spoiled arrogant brats

The whole pack of us
So watching it all?
And thinking it entertains?
Really? Its too much like life.

Used to Be a Rope

The rope around my neck
Just like the kind you see
In those old westerns
Those cowboys on TV
The ropes are long and tangled
They are a mass of blood and skin
All wrapped and twisted
Around the criminals necks and chins
And the toughest part of it all
Is the saga behind them in...
For each one has a story and they all begin.

I was a lonely cowboy
I chose a nice fast horse
I rode a little sideways
More than some of course...
I rode to certain cities
And rode out of them the same
I tricked and kicked and spat
Out the oppressors ugly names...
There was a man of frailty
Character and form
Had none to give him clarity...
No one to keep him warm...
So it was an easy venture
To betray one such as this
And I did it without mention
To any of his kids..
But his oldest ...bless him...
Found out I'd shot his dad...
And he set out to get rich
Set a bounty on my head...
The money it was something..
For in the yesteryear..
A bag of silver jingling
Was a sound all like to hear...

So he found me one late evening
As I knelt beside a stream..
And came up from the shadows
And I? No time to scream...
Offered I come willingly
To the hangman's noose to die
But I threw back a laughing
And punched him in his eye...
He fell hard to the surface
Of the old dry creek bed...
But hustled up quite hurried and
This is what he said...
"You killed my pa, my father..."
"You with him took you know?"
"Six little children's shelter
And they were put out in the snow"
"you forced my mother to ruin...
You forced her now it's true..
She's is now the town's
Laughing stock and lonely prostitute..."
And the kid sat back down on
His heals in the dirt...
I thought he was gonna cry
I could tell his feelings hurt...
"but when you killed him
The night he died they say"
He had a bag of diamonds
That he was trying to sell for wage...

I looked down at the kid...
Squatting on the ground...
And asked quietly of him
His dad's name spit out...

He was called "Franklin see"
But just "Spanky" for short..
He never raised a hand to me
And he never cussed our lord...
His name I guess suited
The man of all I guess

Because he still refuted
Anyone who'd try to mess...
With me or my other siblings
For certain his dear wife..
The man who try to hurt them
Would most surely lose his life...
I gasped for air at the mention
I tried to pretend it brisk
The name without intention
Had proven my brother exists!
I had heard tell the story
Of Mr. "Spanky See"
And how he traded bags of things
From bells to zippers and everything in between
You mean you shot your brother
The kids eyes got bigger then?
And you had no idea of trouble
Of the position you were in??

O my and he sank lower
Than I had seen him do...
"I will tell you this young man...
I will go with you"
"I will get your mother from the tangle
Of the ropes she's in
And I will put it around my own neck
And substitute my chin...
For she has at the violence
Of my hand lost her life
And has given up her home
Her children and caring wife...
So we went on together for the remainder of this trip
And facing wind and weather
It took three weeks or more a bit
But we arrived in Tulsa town
And found the sheriff there
He had a black Tupe' on which
Covered his loss of hair...
He sat and heard the story
Of the man who shot the man

And the kid gladly filled in the details
Of the mother, kids and plans..

The law says there's no
Other way to end this story nope...
But to sling a noose around my neck
And hang me from a rope....
So I here on the platform
Am true to the ended game...
Having not a form fashion or clue
Of why I volunteered or came...

Then from deep within the group
As if muffled in a blanket
A woman in red pushed through
And she protested loud with racket

Let the man go free he is not
The one you need to hang...
For had he not been killed by him...
He would be dead the same....

She pushed and shoved quite forceful
To the wooden platform steps...
She dropped to her knees a beggin'
And in her hands she wept...
Now the rope was loosened..
And removed from over my head..
And it was placed round hers
And was already bloody red...
She gladly hung for all
The day they were hanging me
Because she killed the kids
That had been turned to the street
And you the reader ask
Why did she give up hope?
And I just look at the fact
That around my neck... Used to be a rope.

A Mile in My Shoes

The mile I just asked you to walk?
To feel my pain..to know what I go through?
Well you just barely made it around the block
And I saw your coat tail flapping in the distance
As you went tearing off in the opposite direction...

And the shoes you were trying to trade out with mine are plum so
worn out with your ridicule and judgment I doubt they will even go
past my first toe...

The old saying of walk two moons...and so forth...
Well good grief it has been the middle of next week so far gone now
the moon is a waning crescent...

And the under my skin feeling of knowing what I deal with ?
While you sound very very
Brave
You aren't
Because you have had bot'ox to nicely smooth out the laugh lines and
the
Wisdom lines and the fretting ones
And the weathered ones...
So I am stuck looking old and bearing the lines for both of us....

I thought the other day when you said
"If I can do anything to help..."
You really meant it...
Until we got to the fork in the road and I called you asking for not only
direction but if you would take over for a bit to let me rest...
You just kept on driving..
All
I saw
Was dust
And red taillights....
So now then
How many shoes are in your closet?
And how many moons cross over the night sky and

How many miles you walkin' huh????
Because I just left the hospital with tread marks down the middle of my back and the same old sneakers wiping the same tears
With the same old foundation to fill in and cover over the crying lines...
But hey...
Yea
Catch me on the six o'clock news
You'll see me
I will be the one entering a marathon for you.

We Think We're So Tough

We think we're so tough
We brag about being soldiers
With weapons
And we chant songs
Of victory
But day after day our sword?
Sits on the kitchen counter collecting dust.
Tucked up behind the potholders
And place mats.
Yep, we're tough.
We think we are tough.
We puff ourselves up and out about
Building the poor new houses
And we reach to out to the slums
And we cut their grass.
Then we smile healthily for the local
One horse town newspaper
Hoping the community, camera and clubs
Know we are giving Him the glory!
Yes we are tough.
We snap off the TV. When something "worldly" comes
On in front of our kids and wife..
But when that guy from work sends us that picture of the
Nude woman?
We look just a little bit.
We brag and carry on about how we would be
Beheaded for the cause of the Lord
But we can't even trust him for a furnace or
A bonus
Or a needed couch.
And we think we're tough?
We do.
We sing about his eye being on the sparrow
But we walk around like proud peacocks and
Wise owls.
Both are endangered birds...but those tough little
Sparrows they are everywhere.

They are tough.
Would we be tough if we carried a big stick and
Remembered our leather vests?
Or would we be better off carrying a
Book, the one left behind the potholders,
And cover ourselves with His blood?
We would be tough.

Avoid But Complain

Avoid the drunk
Puking in the alley
Complain about the drunk who
You smell and
Sits behind you at church
Avoid the girl who cuts her arms
Complain about attention getters.
Avoid the women that sleep around
Complain about the preacher with
His boots under their beds.
Avoid the homosexual channel
Complain about the gay neighbor
Avoid the overweight children
Complain about the fast food
Avoid the addicted gambler
Complain about the lost bet on your
Favorite football team.
Avoid but complain
Avoid but complain
When it comes right down to it
We have time for what we want
Money for what we want
And
Tolerance for what we want.
The rest?
Is nothing but belly aching.

Now I Lay Me Down to Sleep

Now I lay me down to sleep
I pray the Lord my soul to keep
If I should die before I wake
I pray the Lord my soul to take.

Sound familiar?

Shouldn't it read something like this?

Now I control every thing in life.
I never rest, sit down or lie.
If one dollar escapes my hand
I know I'd be the weaker man.

The more I see
The more I need
The more I get
The more I fret
And I am not happy not one bit
For if I don't get my way
I throw a fit.

And when I lose my family
And everyone who's close to me
I act shocked to hear the news,
I am so baffled and amused
To hear that everyone has left
So up the corporate ladder take a step.

Welcome to Christianity

Get ready to read some essays on Christians..
We act like the world and believe we are missing

Out on what is going wrong
While we sit in our pews and sing little songs

But oh are we quick to locate a fault!
Not in ourselves or the ways of our walk

But it will be at you that we point our fingers
And it will be how you're wrong and the sins that linger.

And you will never see one of us trading shoes with you
By golly, heck no, the judging 'd be through!!

For if we were to switch and walk just a mile
We would not wear our plastic smiles.

We would not be so full of our supreme vanity.
And if you *still* want to come? Welcome to Christianity!

What About the Calf?

The times we prayed for and we wept
Over the daughter who had calmly slept
In her sin and in her rebellion?
I heard you for months with your yelling.
And the updates on the news was bad
At all the progress the devil had
And what was more now that we laugh
I still have not seen you kill a calf.

When we are sick with sin at our door
And we cry out to Jesus to Christ the Lord
And continue in our deep deep loss
And we cling to the wooden cross
We have given it our all
And there are no more tears to fall
Then one day in the distant view
We see her coming closer too
And we simply throw up a
"Thanks"
To the holy host the God of ranks
And we cant believe how He is baffled
But He doesn't smell the aroma of a calf.
His robe still hangs on a hook
And His ring of son ship is in the crook
Of a box with the rest of jewels
And He is wondering what you're doing?
Because you have just now turned your back
And forgotten all about the calf.
Get the knife or grab the gun
Here come the friends to share the fun
And reap rewards of answered prayer
For without him calves would be everywhere.
And the red robes would take up space
And there would be rings all over the place
But no instead you go on down your path
And you forget to kill the calf.

What Happens When People Aren't Saved

Two men sat heavily down at the bar
The one had come from town
And the other from not
Far
Away.
The first one held his head in his hands....
Said man "I doubt you'd ever understand"
"but if you've got a minute I'll tell you where I
Am..."
The other guy said "save your breath, shut your
Teeth"
"I just laid my wife
Under a
Wreath"
"So nothing you could say could touch my
Grief
Or day"
"I am sorry" the first guy
Replied
"For your wife to so suddenly up and
Die."
And then he hung his head and quietly cried.
Real tears.
"Hey man whats this all about?" The second man
Began to shout
"You didn't know her so cut this out!"
"How dare you act this
Way?"
"Well" said the first "I saw your wife before she was
Born"
"While I was beaten and spat on and scorned"
"I even knew her leg was
Lame....
Long before to this little bar I
Came"
"In fact I helped give her her
Name

Margaret."
The second chap bout' fell off his stool
But regained composure to not lose his cool
And said you've had too much to drink of ol' Charlie's
Brew...
I just know it.
"No" said the first with a drawn out sigh...
It was with reservation that I came here
Tonight...
But your wife insisted that I would find you here
Said that's where you'd been since your wedding
Year
So when she asked if I would
Go
I said only for you I will do it
Though""
"He is so lost and will always be too
If he never even listened to
You."
"Oh" but she said "You know" out
Loud
"That bar is church for a different
Crowd
And the drinks they think they can live forever
And the
Bread they break survives storms and weather
I know if you could just get him to see
How similar they are he'd be sure to
Believe"
At this the man stood up
And waved his
Hands
Come on around here yes
Come here and
Stand
You're about to hear an amazing
Man...

This dude here told of my lame ol lady
He knows how she limped and her name
Why he's
Crazy
But in a minute we'll boot him outta here
And get on with drinkin' our deeply brewed
Beer
But
Then Jesus the son of God and the three in
One
Removed his hat
While
The whole crowd
Came undone
The men and women saw places
Torn
A ring of scars as if made from
Thorns
And then he began to remove his right glove
One woman cried out this is the Christ come down
From above.
Sure enough there were gashes within each of his
Wrists
So deeply chiseled he couldn't make fists
The men all stepped back and some of them bawled
To be so close to the
Son of God
The second man had silently dropped to his
Knees
And all they could hear was him crying
Please
Please
Please
Take me outta here
Away from these tables and all of this
Beer
Then the rest fell down to the ground
And if anyone else had been walking around ?
It would have looked just like a

Mass murder of
Sorts
Instead it was a whole tavern
Receiving the
Lord...
So do not doubt when a Christian is laid in a grave...
Because this is what can happen when people aren't saved.

What Heaven Is Like

Heaven will probably be like Branson Missouri.
All kinds of gospel singing...
The angels with their wash tubs and spoons just a'goin'
Like an old episode of Hee Haw.
Only holier.

And heaven will be like Las Vegas.
All kinds of bright lights and one of a kind concerts
Dancin' and laughin'
Everyone winnin' the jackpot....
Yep it will be like Vegas just
Everyone saved is all.

Heaven will be like the St. Louis science museum.
I can see it now ...
All the molecules and magnets
Carbon dating and ancient squids makin' sense...
Plants and animals sitting around saying...
"I told you so."

I picture heaven like a big ol' Belks or sears
With every possible
Comforter, dining table
Chair or rug
With towels and of course matching wash cloths
The only difference will be
...it's all free.
Comfort cleansing ..
Dining and staying.
And

Finally heaven will a lot like St. Jude's Hospital
With all the kids and wounded adults
The only thing is ..
It will be
Before they're burned.

I have it all pictured this way.
But with or without Belks and museums and towels...
We all need Jesus...since
I just can't picture heaven without him.

What If God Were Faking?

When I was ten I went to a magic show...
The man had a long white beard
A black hat that was long and skinny..and he looked like Abe
Lincoln.....but the things he pulled out of the hat were amazing...live
Cocker Spaniels, doves and I remember counting at least 12 of em'
There was a lamp a suitcase and a glittery fish bowl full of water and
two large orange fish swimming around... And I was old enough to
know better than to believe this stuff that I could see but still young
enough that I believed it anyway...and when I was confronted with my
sin at the age of nineteen I thought back to the little ten year old that
had been tricked by mirrors and black cloths and tables with holes and
optical illusions...and when I accepted christ and was baptized...that
night when I went to sleep I dreamed the worst dream....
There I was at the hill of Golgotha and the sky was splitting in half and
the crowd was chanting 'he saved others lets watch him save himself!!"
And instead of Christ weighed down heavily with the sins of the
world...he began to crack a sly subtle smile...then his eyes flooded
with goofy tears and he snorted right out loud yep he snorted and he
chuckled and the nails bounced rubberly out of his wrists and boing !!
boing!! they bounced down the hillside. And then a mirror was taken
away and what I saw just about floored me there was the waiter from
that great Italian cafe all dressed up like he had just told the biggest
joke....

And I woke up sweaty and full of panic...for I knew that if God faked
His Son's death.. Well...
Hummmm...then He could fake anything... Like love
And rest
And protection
Peace
True inner joy...
Satisfaction from life
Cures
And the list is endless
And the results would be too
And the power would not die....
And when I survey the wondrous cross I did not

See one trick mirror and not one black top hat
What wore me out was the way he was suspended in
The air...
Wonder about faking that.

What If He Said....

To the blind man before he healed....
What if Christ said, "I'll make you a deal."
I'll tell you what I want you to find...
All the reasons you think you are blind.
And when you make a list of all those....
Find me and we'll review them I suppose.

Then as he walked away
The blind man said,"there just ain't no way..
For me to make a list of anything.
I don't know why I was born not seeing
Now where did He go what should I do?
He was my last hope when passing through.

Did Jesus say to those in jail...
"Hey dude, you post at least half the bond at least half of the bail?
In fact you got yourself in there let's see you get out
Now don't start this crying stuff and you better not shout..
And to the naked man running around...
Did he say "Bet the next time you won't listen to satan's growl.

He never said I"ll tell what do
You just straighten up...quit acting a fool
Now if you'll just get dressed and get a new gig...
I won't have to kill all these fine fatted pigs...
Why ...everyone thinks you are crazy enough
But if you'll get it together you may just call their bluff.

And to the woman at the well that noon...
I'd help you if you 'd stop sleeping around you could...
Have a cute little house on the outskirts of town...
And if you worked harder than ever, and toil the ground...
Then I would do my share to further your plans..
And may even throw in another hus-band.

Before each miracle did Christ make us work?
Proving to him what we think we are worth?
Did he say first this and then this from me?
Did he want a report of our finances before he hung from the tree?
I wonder oh when did we see it the this way...
That we have to be good enough for him to hear us pray?

I witness his love his mercy and grace
And it doesn't come just because I have a clean face.
He doesn't extend his forgiveness to man
If we'd all get together and save rubber stamps...
He lays no conditions on when he defends
And has never no never said, that it all depends....

So when I check myself and do not compare
My worth with others because it isn't fair...
He knows we are all wicked
And that is the truth....
All born in sin carried out throughout youth....
He blesses and bless and will do it again
But it's not because we're good no it's all about Him.

What the Devil Meant

This was the hardest case ever.
Tammy had counseled for 12 years
But this one---bad.
She bowed her head to prepare her mind
And ask for words

She didn't quite finish when she heard
The door open
So she quickly said "amen" and then
"come in".
Escorted by two six foot something police guards
Was this skinny teenager.
Peter was his name and the information about him?
Unending.

Abused by both parents as a baby
And beat by both the rest of the time
He stood there with rage and revenge
For the people who brought him to talk to this woman.

Talk about what? He thought.
What would she know about the junk
I have been through?
She had that white skirt on and little vest ..
Probably her BMW they passed out in the parking lot.
"so she said
Where you from?
The darker side of hell mam.
He said mam with deep sarcasam
Well then maybe we will start there.
She said
Can you tell me why you are here?
Nope
Then you're good to go huh?
His eyes lit up
No by law you have a two week course
To complete. Sounds like a movie I saw once

No no movie
This is real she said.
Are you familiar with the bible?
His face twitched
The Bible she repeated
You have heard of God's word haven't you?
Look lady I don't believe in that anymore
God and his powerful love
I just wonder why He did not show up
Or where was He huh?
She went through her favorite passages about God.
They were out of time
So she said
What the devil meant for evil God means for good
And calls things alive even thought they look dead. Remember it was
not God who was behind all this.
Over the next two weeks
They talked on and on about abuse
And healing and about God
and his ways and each session
She ended it by saying what
The devil meant for evil the Lord God meant for good
And calls things alive even though
They appear dead.
But she saw him at her door the
Monday of the third week then the fourth and finally each day for two
years
She asked him you are at the place where you need to make a decision
What he a was surprised...about God.
Oh him well after that a first week I accepted him as my savior.
Not because of all the scripture
Or the prayers
No not from church members
Or the law forcing me to come it was the first time you said that thing
about the devil meaning evil ..
I thought about it a lot.
Then when you said
God calls things alive even though they look dead...I started to forgive.
I forgave my parents

I forgave em and left it alone.
I am healed and free I am clean.
I have been listening
And it all makes sense.
'Well" said Tammy
A boys home just opened up on the corner of 7th and third they only take the severe
The impossible
The most serious abuse
neglect
Violence and drugs even felons.
These kids are young too young for prison
And this clinic is a last ditch effort to restore them to society.
They asked if there was anyone from this clinic who could go to mentor
To counsel not professionally but someone who they can get close to can trust and talk to.

I was wondering ...
Yes he said
Before she could finish... It took peter two years to heal
but within the next two years he touched every single kid.
Prayed over every case
Spoke truth over every head
And laid his own story out for all to see
To hear
To touch
To know

And every single day he closed out his sessions by looking the kid in his eyes and saying

What the devil meant for evil God means for good and calls alive things that appear dead

.those two years of counseling ended up producing five evangelical preachers seven bible college students and at least 10 to 12 kids leading bible study in their schools

All of us were dead
all.
Appeared to have no hope
No friend to save
No rescue
No strength
And then along comes someone.
They know us
See us
And still love us.
And with each breath we are restored because they lay their lives out

the devil will always mean things for evil and God will always mean
them for good but for the calling things alive even though they appear
dead? Well the devil will never do what God did the very first week of
creation.
took a lump of mud and a rib
And even though they appeared dead
"He called them to life"
And He's been doing it ever since

Who ?

I heard the dog barking
I threw the covers back and let my feet hit the cold wood
Grabbed my tattered robe and went to see what had stirred the dog
up...
To my surprise I saw twenty or so sparrows standing and flitting some
hovering and others just looking on...while a man
In white
Fed them...

I heard the bell ringing
I threw my books in my locker and hit the halls
Grabbed my coat and went to see what was going on..
To my surprise I saw twenty or so of the poorest kids in school
standing
And limping some sitting and others craning necks to catch a glimpse
Of a man
In white
Talking to them

A woman older now
Had just suffered a fall...
Broken leg
Just got her crutches from the hospital
She wasn't sturdy on them yet...
And who do you suppose was teaching her?
The man in white
That's who.

And the man knows no time...
Sparrows always need food...

And He knows no schedule
The poor don't have one either...

When I walked home
I crawled back into bed.
The dog had settled down...

And I
Saw him
All in white
Walking away...
With my crutches slung over his shoulder
I leaned against the closet
Draped my tattered robe on the chair
Tucked my head
Under a feathered wing

Windows Everywhere

They say when God closes a door
He always opens a window....

But today I have to beg to differ...

The news of her death left the door
Slammed shut...

After a moment of stunned silence
We began looking around for some windows...

But there weren't any.

And I remember the time the truck driver
Picked up the man and woman looking all poor

They robbed him

They killed him ....the window
Had been boarded up
Long ago.

The small business my granddaddy owned
Back in the thirties

Went through the first two years of the depression
Feeding folks, handing out jobs, even letting the

Have-nots hang around

Then the dishwasher came after we had all
Gone home and with the knife he had
So carefully washed..

He cruelly stuck it into my granddaddy's chest
No one had thought to look in or out of a window
That night.

Illnesses, drought, cancer, heart failure, engine failures, flat tires, no
hires, retires, nursing homes, homeless ones, too young to die, too old
to live....
And you know?
Not one of them checked for an open window.

Sometimes when God closes a door...the windows stay glued shut
too....
And Then When You Least Expect It
The friend of the girl who dies named her own baby girl after her...
She grew to reach her whole seventh grade class for the Lord.
Of those who were saved...a third of the boys grew to be men who went
onto the mission field..
There was one who researched the very cancer the woman that the girl
was named after had.
And he found the cure.
Even opened up his own clinic....
Called it "open window".

And the trucker, along with my granddaddy....?
They each had bibles in their back seats.

Turns out the one that buried my granddaddy
Was kin in a round about way to the man who stabbed him...
He set up a college trust fund....
To honor small business men ...starting up ministry type stores...
Called it the 'open window" scholarship.

He has come to make all things new,
Clean clocks
Re-thread needles
Retrain horses
Rethink death
Revive
Retie

Rehire
And restore...
The homeless have homes
The cars have doors
And they come equipped with doors
And windows....Everywhere.

Worthy

He knew about the drinking problems 6.5 billion of us would have
The porn and exploitation problems that 6.5 billion more would
succumb to
He knew molestation would destroy our girls and
He knew the sin would spill over to our boys in time ...
It has.
He was not sitting idle while you and your spouse divide
Property and visiting hours
And He knew your best friend would take her life at the age of 20
He wasn't caught unaware the millions of times
Tears fell
From millions
Either from being caught
Or not in
Sin
And prisons boast of the tormented
Captives that did unspeakable things
To infants and mothers and the old
And now they turn on themselves and torture
Creases their brows and their hearts are no longer pumping
Real blood....
And the needy cry out
The poor
The weak
The uneducated
The lame, mal-nourished, the deaf and the blind
All ban together
And walk into walls
And spew out death wishes
To the rest of us who think we
Can walk and speak and feed ourselves from borrowed
Silver spoons.

Worthy is He

Worthy is the one who is blamed for it all but
Came anyway
Who died anyway
Who bled
Who cried out
Forgive
Forgive
Forgive
Take me
Instead
And we did
We did
Take him.
And still do.
Take blessings as if they
Are expectations
And promises
As if they are deserved things
And sufferings as if they are
Surprises and we fling them away
And shift our feet and scratch our heads
And justify our sin
And we cease from suffering and lay back
In Lazyboy recliners and flip the remote to watch the news
Where we witness
.....sufferings.
And some poor, lame, helpless, nobody
Lifts his dirty hands to the heavens and gives credit for the
Blessings of having his shack being swept up and away from this earth
For his picture album of grand-kids that his Aunt Mavis quilted in
blue with green trim was shredded
And the mother dying with cancer leaving two sons
One three
And one thirteen.
She leaves a note behind explaining the blessing of death and leaves
them a legacy of
Suffering in graceful admonition of a high God

Who
Did
It
Too
She is one of those rare persons
Worthy of sitting at the feet of a savior who
Is holy
Who is
Worthy of every breath
Every utterance
And every
Suffered moment
Because He came
Anyway
Displayed for our mocking
And our ridicule
And our spit
Out slaps of curses
He came anyway
And cries out forgive
Forgive
Forgive
He is worthy
Through it all
Healing bringing flowers for graves and weddings and church pews
He did it with our blame of Him hanging like necklaces and lipstick
kisses of betrayal
Worthy is he
Because
He was the only one worthy
To come
Big enough to make it all bow
And worthy of the glory it would cause
He knew it
He came anyway.

There Were Movies in the Bible

The **Red Dragon** fell
With a **Shrek**
From the **Precious**
League of Extraordinary Gentlemen,
And of all the
Little Women
To be **The Bourne Identity**
Of **The Good Shepherd**,
He, **The Uninvited**,
The Illusionist,
Began a **Battle Royale**
Against **Little Miss Sunshine.**
It was like the
Slum Dog Millionaire
And **The Gangs of New York**
Against the
Children of the Corn.
And
When Cain killed Abel
He must have cried out
O Brother Where Art Thou?
But when **Superman Returns**
With a seemingly
Mission Impossible,
The Prophet shows
The Bucket List of all
The Incredibles
Who will come after him.
Then **The Perfect Storm**
Hits **Planet terror**
And then **The Hurt Locker**
Really begins.
There are many
Stories in the bible,
Stories about
The Descent,
And **Oceans Eleven**

And **The Big Fish** are a few.
We read of moses as a baby,
As he is placed in the
Mystic River by **Public Enemies**.
He is **Taken** at
Twilight by a
Hellraiser with
Paranormal Activity.
Love Actually
Comes from this and the
Lord of the Rings
Gathers soldiers to go
Into the Wild to
Fight for **Pride and Prejudice**.
The Transformers
Walk **8 mile** to the desert.
One day they look **Up**
To the mount where it
Seemed they would see a
Dead Man Walking...
But when **Dr. Strangelove** Moses
Returned it was nothing but
The Good the Bad and the Ugly
Involved with **Sin City**.
The **Hills Have Eyes**
And **the Dark Knight**
Began his **Walk to Remember**
Back up the mount.
But old habits **Die Hard**
And the new testament just gets
Dumb and Dumber.
Then
The new testament shows
Us **The Bourne Ultimatim**
And **The Bourne Supremacy**
Come to earth from
The **Star Trek** and
The Kingdom of Heaven.
The Strangers are among

Natural Born Killers
And soon it is obvious
This is **No Country for Old Men.**
The two young people are
Sleepless in Seattle
But their **Passion of the Christ**
Allows for a **Shawshank Redemption.**
I know there are over **300**
Names in **The Notebook,**
And even though the
Wedding Crashers
Cause his church to
Look like the **Body of Lies**
He can still take
The Blind Side of
The Enemy of the State
And gather his people
As the great **The Collector**
And **The Itailian Job** is
Finally **The Terminal** end.
I've read
The Fantastic Four gospels that
Lead us all the way to
Revelation where
He signs the book with
P.s. I Love You.
One day we will be
The Departed
With him in glory
And will witness
The **Apocalypse Now.**
But don't look for me here because

I'll be **Gone Baby Gone**.

Mean to Say Mothers?

At the time coming in to set the table was such a pain
and going to bed ..missing "Laugh In" and "The Carol Burnette Show"
I doubted I would ever forgive her.
Her view on my choices of friends
saying,"No" to me sleeping over at certain girls houses...she could have cared less
how many times I rolled my eyes.
The ways she always took turns praying around the circle was so childish to me
And she always had some stupid coupon for a deal that was already a bargain..
so how dumb was that.
Not dating until age sixteen..I told her all the good guys would be taken.
Not letting me smart off to my dad
even though I knew she was frustrated too?
She still would not have it.
She never made us late for anything.
She always came to anything I ever did or was a part of.
She bought tickets, sold tickets promoted, cared about bragged about
cried over, wept over prayed about everything I ever did.
So O God Why did You say to inherit the kingdom we must become like children?
Didn't You mean to Say Mothers?

She Sat in My Car

She sat there in my car. Brisk Friday morning that it was, us goin' no where really. She turns to me and says " You know when I was twelve I got baptized."

"Oh," I said "That's nice".

But you don' understand she went on to say....it was so my dad would not abuse me like he did my sisters. I thought if I were covered in Jesus he could not hurt me.

I cringed to hear the rest.

"But he did anyway."

I knew it, I thought to myself, I knew it.

How do you get people to see it isn't the 'being spared' from all wrong that displays God's mighty power....it's the ability to save ANYWAY that is what shows His power the most.

So here I am sitting with her in my car trying to tell her this ...then all of a sudden she turns to me again and says,

"My name means 'angel'" "I know because I looked it up one time when I was twelve"

"Then that should bring you comfort" I said

"It never did until now....."

"Because now, I have met one....and now I know He will protect me and help me heal..."

And it is funny you know....

Her sitting in my car looking out of my dirty car windows....

She was actually doing it....really.

Looking at Him through windows of
STAINED GLASS.

Authors Notes

While writing this book I have felt the rush of God's mercy strong. In every page and over every story He has placed a smile. He is truly the truth, and living life. He is the notes, lyrics, harmony and melody to any song that is sung from a throat. I have seen Him come out of nowhere when I cry, and hover close even when a cry is too hard to utter. God is bigger than we think, more real than the book you hold, and is coming again. You maybe thinking "he isn't coming back." "It's all a scare tactic." But I ask you this one thing....

What if it's all true?

What if you did not accept Him because of pride, or ego, money or power?

What if all this time His way was right and clean and good and you missed out on it?

You know something dear friend, Jesus Saves..and I end with this last story.

Jesus Saves

On the front page of the newspaper, there were the headlines "JESUS SAVES".

Evidently, a man in New Mexico named Jesus Martinez rushed into a burning building and led 288 people to safety. He braved the burning building and smoke emerging as a hero. The fire crew carried him around on their shoulders, and the mayor honored him at a public ceremony.

And as I read this story, I thought about another man named Jesus. He did some of the same things. Rushed into a burning smoke filled world and carried the entire world to safety. He was brave and tough. The reception did not go the way it did for the man in the news. He was not honored at all. He was spit on and mocked, cast down and betrayed. He was not carried around on shoulders, but instead He carried our sins on His.

I reflected on this. And in the end decided truly the newpaper was right.

Jesus Saves.....Jesus Saves.....yes oh yes my Jesus Saves

The End